AQUATIC
EXERCISE

The Jones and Bartlett Series in Health Sciences

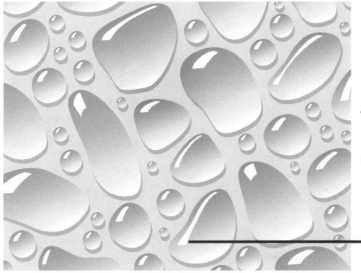

AQUATIC
EXERCISE

Ruth Sova, M.S.
Aquatic Exercise Association

Jones and Bartlett Publishers
Boston   London

Editorial, Sales, and Customer Service Offices
Jones and Bartlett Publishers
One Exeter Plaza
Boston, MA 02116

Jones and Bartlett Publishers International
P.O. Box 1498
London W6 7RS
England

Library of Congress Cataloging-in-Publication Data
Sova, Ruth.
    Aquatic exercise / Ruth Sova.
      p.   cm.
    Includes bibliographical references.
    ISBN 0-86720-754-X
    1. Aquatic exercises. 2. Aquatic exercises--Therapeutic use.
I. Title.
GV838.53.E94S665 1992
613.7'16--dc20   92–18243
                                              CIP

Copyeditor: Alyce Dubec
Design and Production: Karen Mason
Cover Design: David Kelley
Prepress: The Courier Connection
Printing and Binding: Courier Westford

Photo credits:

Kurt J. Sova, photographer

Companies: Aquatic Fitness Products and HydroFit

The author does not necessarily endorse any of the products or associations discussed in this book.

Printed in the United States of America
97 96 95 94 93   10 9 8 7 6 5 4 3 2 1

CONTENTS

PREFACE

Aquatic exercise is the most exciting, effective, and exhilarating way to work out. I am thrilled that you are involved in my favorite way to fitness.

The aquatics industry is growing and changing quickly, and the rapid growth challenges us to remain informed. A knowledge base like the one presented in this book will help us to move safely and effectively toward positive results.

Aquatic exercisers must have a wide spectrum of knowledge to work out safely in the pool. This book has been written to be a thorough resource to answer this need.

We can learn from problems encountered by other fitness industries. Overuse injuries have occurred in both joggers and aerobic dancers. What can we do to protect ourselves? Enthusiasts in any segment of the fitness industry have always faced particular problems. What can we do to protect ourselves from chronic exposure to heat and humidity? What about our unique environment? What is the safest program for someone with a bad back? What exercises can obese children perform?

Since it is difficult to be an authority on every topic, I found specialists to review each section. I want to thank this diverse group. Dani Riposo assisted with the fitness concepts and is widely quoted in the nutrition section.

Alison Osinski reviewed the safety issues, and Bud Sova and Jack Wasserman assisted with the biomechanics of aqua physics. Vicki Chossek, Peg Windhorst, and Joanna Midtlying, reviewed material content, and Karl Knopf, June Lindle, Julie See, and Angie Nelson gave editorial advice. Mr. Jun Konno also reviewed content with an international perspective. Varied aquatic equipment manufacturers provided us with photographs. The Aquatic Exercise Association, Vicki Chossek, Dani Riposo, and Nicole Sova provided technical assistance.

In addition to the technical support, I would like to thank the following for their valuable assistance: Karen Mason, Graphic Design and Production Services, for assistance with the book's production; Nicole Sova for transcribing the manuscript; Kurt Sova for the photography; Bud Sova for financial support; the Aquatic Exercise Association staff, Vicki Chossek, and the Jalkanen family for their support; Alyce Dubec for help editing the manuscript; and Joe Burns, editor and vice president of Jones and Bartlett Publishers, for assistance with this book.

Because of all their help, this book is a comprehensive reference tool for each of us to use as we exercise, buy new equipment, or have any specific questions about aquatics.

AQUATIC EXERCISE

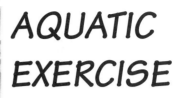

AQUATIC EXERCISE

Chapter One

OVERVIEW

The concept of aquatic exercise is an idea whose time has certainly come. The jogging craze of the late sixties and seventies, the aerobic dance frenzy of the seventies and early eighties, and the pursuit of total fitness through cross training that brings us into the nineties have matured into an intelligent pursuit of health and fitness. Exercise is the fountain of youth, and everyone wants to drink from it.

Like almost everything in life, jogging, aerobic dance, and cross training have proven to be less than perfect. As more people have joined in the bouncing, jumping, jogging, and pumping, reports of minor injuries have become more frequent. The impact experienced during these sports has created countless exercise dropouts. As Baby Boomers move into middle age, they are demanding a fitness program that will enable them to continue exercising for the rest of their lives, despite joint problems and reduced flexibility they may eventually experience.

Thus, aquatic exercise has become a major exercise alternative in our fitness-conscious society. It is a perfect mix of water and workout. Since the movements are performed in chest-deep water, these programs appeal to the swimmer and nonswimmer alike.

The buoyant support of the water effectively cancels approximately 90% of the weight of a person submerged to the neck. This dramatically decreases compression stress on weight-bearing joints, bones, and muscles. Since it is thought that most movements done in the water involve only concentric muscular contractions, muscle soreness is minimal. The possibility of muscle, bone, and joint injuries is almost completely eliminated. Individuals concerned with excess pressure on their ankles, knees, hips, and back can now increase their strength, flexibility, and cardiovascular endurance with safe aerobics: aquatic exercise.

Buoyancy makes the program ideal for many people who have painful joints or weak leg muscles and cannot participate in alternative exercise programs. Special populations—such as those with arthritis or other joint problems, obesity, and back problems, as well as pre- and postnatal women, sedentary individuals, and those recovering from injury or surgery—are prime candidates for aquatic exercise.

With the body submerged in water, blood circulation automatically increases to some extent. Water pressure on the body also helps to promote deeper ventilation (breathing) of the lungs. With a well-planned activity, both circulation and ventilation increase even more.

Flexibility work is increased and performed more easily in water because of the lessened gravitational pull. It is much easier to do leg straddles or side stretches in water. Many individuals can do leg bobbing or jogging in water who could never do so on land. The resistant properties of water also make it a perfect exercise medium for the well-conditioned individual who is looking to accomplish more in less time. The resistance of the water makes taking a simple walk a challenging workout, testing muscular endurance and strength and cardiorespiratory fitness. Vigorous water exercise can make a major contribution to individual flexibility, muscular strength and endurance, body composition, and cardiorespiratory fitness.

There are many kinds of aquatic exercise programs to choose from. This book describes many and offers sample programs. Variations can be made by combining or alternating programs to suit an individual's specific needs.

In this book, the term **aquatic aerobics** or water exercise will refer to vertical exercise in the water with the participant submerged to chest or shoulder depth. Most aquatic exercisers stand in chest-deep water or work out vertically in the deep end (diving well) of the pool while using buoyant devices.

OVERALL FITNESS

Overall **fitness** may be defined as a combination of physical, mental, and emotional well-being. It implies a positive outlook on life with enough strength and stamina to perform daily tasks with energy to spare for leisure pursuits.

Hypokinetic Disease

For reasons we are just beginning to understand, physical fitness is related to overall fitness and total well-being in a variety of ways. Unfortunately, our society is largely sedentary, which conflicts with the inherent purpose of our bodies, namely, that they are designed for movement.

Movement helps to keep us healthy. Without movement, our bodies begin to deteriorate. Sometimes that deterioration is mistakenly chalked up to age instead of disuse. The deterioration that results from inactivity has caused a whole new syndrome of disease in our society, diseases that are hypokinetic. **Hypokinetic disease** is a condition caused by or aggravated by inactivity. (*Hypo* means "not enough." *Kinetic* means "movement.")

Common examples of hypokinetic disease are heart disease, back pain, obesity, ulcers, and blood vessel diseases, such as atherosclerosis. Hypokinetic mental disorders include insomnia, lethargy, depression, and anxiety. Hypokinetic diseases also include metabolic disorders, such as adult-onset diabetes and hypoglycemia; bone and joint disorders, such as osteoporosis and osteoarthritis; and the stress disorders of constipation and mood swings.

The physically fit person, besides having a reduced risk of hypokinetic disease, is more likely than his or her unfit neighbor to feel good, look good, and enjoy life. He or she can work and play more effectively; is more creative; and is less likely to suffer from anxiety, depression, and psychosomatic illness.

Mind and Body

The mind-body connection in overall fitness works in reverse also. That is, the emotionally stable person with a positive attitude will be less likely to suffer from physical diseases. Dr. Thomas McKeown, a prominent English physician, said, "It is now evident that the health of man is determined predominantly, not by medical intervention, but, by his behavior, his food, and the nature of the world in which he finds himself" (Conrad, 1979, pp. 30–31). Practicing muscular and mental relaxation techniques, visualization, self-responsibility, cognitive concepts, imagery, and positive affirmations will all help in gaining overall fitness.

Mental Attitude

The mental attitude of the regular exerciser is improved not only by a psychological phenomenon but also by a physical one. While the exact effects of powerful hormones called *endorphins* are not clear yet, they seem to be related to pain, emotions, the immune system, exercise, and the reproduction system. The feelings of well-being that come with vigorous exercise have been traced to endorphins. They also may have an effect on mental problems. For instance, patients experiencing depression often have low levels of endorphins.

Mental Sharpness

The mind-body connection also correlates with mental sharpness, alertness, and sometimes intelligence. A study at Purdue University found that after working out three times a week for six months, one group was not only 20% fitter but scored 70% higher in a test of complex decision making (Welch, 1989).

Overall fitness should be a goal for all people. This book will cover aspects of the physical portion of fitness. It is a guide to achieving physical fitness through water exercise.

PHYSICAL FITNESS

Major Components of Physical Fitness

There are five major aspects or components of physical fitness:

1. Cardiorespiratory endurance
2. Muscular strength
3. Muscular endurance
4. Flexibility
5. Body composition

When working toward physical fitness, many people include only one or two of these five aspects in their workout plan. All five components are interrelated yet separate enough that a person can be fit in one aspect but not in the others. A truly fit person will include all aspects of physical fitness in his or her workout and will be fit in each one.

Cardiorespiratory Endurance

Cardiorespiratory endurance, or fitness, involves the ability of the heart and blood to supply oxygen from the respiratory system to the cells of the body during sustained exercise. To increase this component of physical fitness, aerobic exercise must take place.

In order to be aerobic, the exercise must be continuous, involve the body's large muscles (the quadriceps, hamstrings, and gluteals in the legs and buttocks), and last for at least 20 minutes. An individual should work at a perceived exertion level of "somewhat hard" to "hard" and/or elevate the heartrate into the working zone. (See Chapter 5 for more information on heartrates and perceived exertion.) To improve cardiorespiratory endurance, an aerobic workout should be repeated at least three times a week. Leaping, kicking, jogging, and walking in the water will increase the workload on the cardiorespiratory system so that endurance benefits can be obtained.

Exercise is usually associated with its cardiac benefits. A recent study has shown that lack of exercise may be the single risk factor most clearly associated with future coronary disease (Riposo, 1985). Regular cardiorespiratory exercise has been shown to improve, to varying degrees, almost all of the commonly accepted risk factors that can be changed: lack of exercise, elevated cholesterol, elevated triglycerides, lowered high-density lipoproteins

DIAGRAM 1–1 Primary Risk Factors for Coronary Heart Disease

1. Hypertension (high blood pressure)
2. High blood lipids and cholesterol levels
3. Cigarette smoking
4. Obesity (overweight)
5. Family history of heart disease (close blood relative died suddenly before age of 55 or family history of high cholesterol, Marfan's syndrome, or enlarged heart)
6. Atherosclerosis (hardening of the arteries)
7. Diabetes
8. Sedentary lifestyle (lack of physical activity)
9. Stress
10. Age (women, risk greater after menopause; men, risk increases proportionately with age)
11. Sex (men more at risk than women until age of 50–60, then both are equal)

(HDL), hypertension, smoking, obesity, stress, and diabetes (glucose metabolism). Myocardial efficiency is also markedly improved, as evidenced by decreased resting pulse and decreased heartrate at the same workload during exercise. This means that after doing a specific workout program for about eight weeks, the body adapts, making it easier for an individual to do that same program. The effect of

DIAGRAM 1–2 Secondary Risk Factors for Coronary Heart Disease

1. Asthma or other allergies
2. Arthritis or other joint problems
3. Anxiety
4. Use of medications, alcohol, drugs
5. Current activity
6. Recent surgery
7. Previous difficulty with exercise (chest discomfort, dizziness, extreme breathlessness)
8. Pregnancy status

exercise on the heart alone makes it a valuable prescription for both physicians and patients (see Diagrams 1–1 and 1–2).

Muscular Strength

Muscular strength is the ability of a muscle to exert great force in a single effort. It is usually attained by lifting weights. To achieve muscular strength, each muscle group works submaximally (about 60% of the maximum ability) for about eight repetitions. After all muscle groups have been worked, the entire workout is repeated once or twice.

Water offers a natural resistance or weight. Paddles, water-tight weights, webbed gloves, and special weight-training equipment can all be used to intensify the force of the workload in the water.

Muscular Endurance

Muscular endurance is the ability of a muscle to repeat a contraction with a moderate workload over a long period of time. Ten to thirty repetitions of any movement build up endurance rather than strength. A workout involving 10 repetitions working each muscle group can be done three times.

Muscular endurance and toning can be achieved sooner with the water's resistance than with endurance workouts on land. Moreover, there is minimal risk of injury due to the cushioning effect of the water.

Flexibility

Flexibility is the ability of limbs to move the joints through a normal range of motion. Flexibility workouts include static stretching of each major muscle group for 30 to 60 seconds. Only muscles should be stretched, not tendons or ligaments.

Due to the lessened effect of gravity in the water, the joints can be moved through a wider range of motion without excess pressure, and long-term flexibility can be achieved.

Body Composition

Body composition is the proportion of fat body mass to lean body mass. It should not be confused with being overweight or underweight, since it does not deal with weight. In fact, eliminating fat body mass and increasing lean body mass may increase the total body weight. A desirable amount of body fat for women is 18% to 20%. The well-conditioned female athlete normally has 16% to 18% body fat. Men should have 10% to 12% body fat. Male athletes usually achieve 7% to 8% body fat.

The average person burns 450 to 700 calories while performing one hour of aerobic exercise. In the water, 77% of the calories burned come from fat stores, thus reducing the fat mass in a body. Muscle tissue (lean body mass) growth is stimulated while moving through the water resistance.

Minor Components of Physical Fitness

Other components of fitness listed by sports physiologists are called minor components or skill-related components. Skill-related fitness is related to performing motor skills, such as playing soccer or walking a tightrope. The skill-related components of physical fitness are:

- —**Speed**—the ability to perform a movement in a short period of time
- —**Power**—the ability to transfer energy into force at a fast rate (a combination of strength and speed in one explosive action)
- —**Agility**—the ability to rapidly and accurately change the position of the entire body
- —**Reaction time**—the amount of time elapsed between stimulation and reaction to that stimulation
- —**Coordination**—the integration of separate motor activities in the smooth, efficient execution of a task
- —**Balance**—the maintenance of equilibrium while stationary or moving (static and dynamic balance).

All of the fitness components, both health-related and skill-related aspects, are trainable; that is, they will show improvement when subjected to appropriate activity.

Principles of Exercise

Six basic principles of exercise must be understood in order to create a sound exercise program:

1. Overload
2. Progressive overload
3. Adaptation
4. Specificity
5. Reversibility
6. Variability

Overload

The **overload** principle states that if an increase in demands is made on a muscle or system, that body part will respond by *adapting* to the increase. If adequate rest and good nutrition accompany the overload, there will be an increase in strength or efficiency. Improvement cannot occur unless overload is present. Training occurs by means of the overload principle.

Progressive Overload

Progressive overload is also sometimes called progressive resistance. It is the principle of gradually increasing overload. If the overload or stress is increased too quickly, injury, pain, or exhaustion may result instead of proper training. "No pain, no gain" is a fallacy. Only in competitive athletics, where participants are willing to take enormous risks for the possibility of superior performance, does this slogan have any merit, and even then, it is questionable.

All training of exercise programs should follow the principle of progressive overload. Trying to do too much, too soon paves the way for exhaustion, pain, and possible injury. Programs should begin at low intensity, for a short duration, with minimum frequency, and gradually increase the overload in each category. Training occurs by means of the overload principle.

Adaptation

Adaptation is also called *training*. It is an improvement in the fitness level that results when the body adapts to overload. Place greater work demands on a muscle (including the heart) than it is used to performing, and it will respond by getting stronger. Stretch a muscle longer than it is accustomed to being stretched, and it will become more flexible. Expose muscles to sustained activity for longer than they are accustomed to, and muscular endurance will increase.

The body will adapt to the stresses or overload placed on it so that an increase in overload can be made. By the same token, if the overload is less than normal for a specific component of fitness, there will be a decrease in that particular component. Keeping the overload at a constant level will maintain the current level of fitness.

Specificity

The principle of **specificity** states that only the muscle, body part, or system that is being overloaded will adapt and improve. Thus, a stretching program will not improve cardio-respiratory fitness. Just as overload is specific to each component of fitness, it is also specific to each body part. Those muscle groups being overloaded are the only ones that develop. Weight training for the hamstrings will do nothing for the biceps.

In order to see improvements in all the major components of fitness, the program has to be designed specifically to overload each component. In order to have muscle balance in a workout, the workout must be designed to involve all the muscles equally.

Reversibility

Reversibility means that fitness benefits cannot be stored by the body. Several days without a workout means the training level will start to decline. It is generally thought that it takes 12 weeks to improve the fitness level and only 2 weeks to see it decline.

Variability

Variability is a principle that most people ignore. It states that adaptation or fitness improvements are enhanced by varying the intensity, length, or type of workout. Variability adds to the training effect.

The popular fitness concept of **cross training** uses variability as its foundation. Athletes who have hit fitness plateaus have been able to move to higher levels of fitness through cross training. Rather than do the same fitness activity for every workout, athletes do different types of workouts on different days. Runners can use deep-water running, biking, and water strength training to increase their fitness levels. Swimmers can use cross-country skiing, water walking, and weight lifting. Any change in the type, intensity, or length of the workout will enhance fitness improvements.

Reasons for cross training include:

—an optimal development of all components of physical fitness
—an enhanced motivation toward exercise adherence
—injury prevention due to avoidance of overtraining
—development of balance with opposing muscle groups
—effectiveness in weight-loss programs
—an overall increase in general physical fitness

All training or adaptation works on the principle of stressing the body and letting it recover in a stronger form. Too often, exercisers make the mistake of repeating the same workout, day after day. That can stress the same muscles and joints until an injury occurs.

In designing an exercise program to provide maximum physical and mental health benefits, activities to promote all the major components of fitness should be included. Cardiovascular work should be integral to the program, since cardiovascular fitness is most important for total well-being. Strength and flexibility work enable people to perform their daily tasks with ease, as well as help protect them from back pain. Body composition can be favorably altered by endurance and strength training.

Many of the skill-related fitness components can also be included in a basic exercise program. We know that if a person's goal is to improve in a particular sport, training in the specific fitness components and movement coordinations of that sport are necessary for optimum improvement. Nevertheless, it is easy to incorporate into a series of exercise routines movements to improve speed, agility, reaction time, balance, and coordination with a resultant improvement in overall fitness.

Taking time at the end of each exercise session for conscious voluntary relaxation is important. Slow stretches and guided relaxation add a feeling of mental and physical release that has also been shown to have important health benefits.

KEY WORDS

Aquatic aerobics
Buoyancy
Fitness
Hypokinetic disease
Cardiorespiratory endurance
Muscular strength
Muscular endurance
Flexibility

Body composition
Speed
Power
Agility
Reaction time
Coordination
Balance

Overload
Progressive overload
Adaptation
Specificity
Reversibility
Variability
Cross training

SUMMARY

- The concept of aquatic exercise is an idea whose time has come.
- Exercise is the fountain of youth, and everyone wants to drink from it.
- The buoyant support of the water effectively cancels approximately 90% of the weight of a person submerged to the neck.
- Flexibility work is increased and performed more easily in water because of the lessened gravitational pull.
- There are five major components of physical fitness: cardiorespiratory endurance, muscular strength, muscular endurance, flexibility, and body composition.
- Minor components of physical fitness are: speed, power, agility, reaction time, coordination, and balance.
- Six basic principles of exercise are: overload, progressive overload, adaptation, specificity, reversibility, and variability.
- Minor components of physical fitness are: speed, power, agility, reaction time, coordination, and balance.
- Taking time at the end of each exercise session for conscious voluntary relaxation is important.

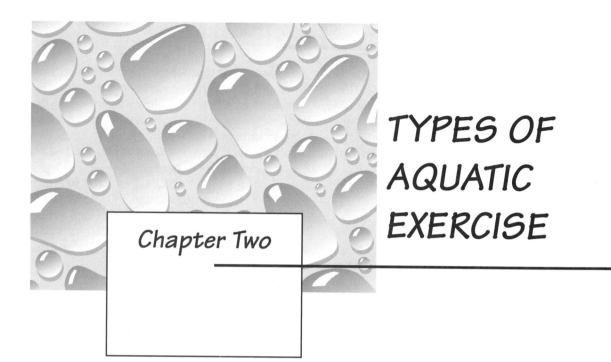

TYPES OF AQUATIC EXERCISE

Chapter Two

The format of aquatic exercise programs varies, depending on their goals. Almost any program or program variation follows either the aerobic or nonaerobic class format. Programs focusing on cardiorespiratory conditioning, such as water aerobics, water walking, deep-water programs, and circuit training, follow the *aerobic* class format. Programs that focus on muscular endurance, strength, or flexibility follow a *nonaerobic* class format.

FORMAT FOR CARDIORESPIRATORY-CONDITIONING CLASSES

Warm-Up

The **warm-up** is a combination of three different class segments that increase body temperature. The warm-up allows the exerciser to safely exercise at a high intesity. Water cardiorespiratory (aerobic) classes usually begin with a warm-up lasting 5 to 10 minutes. Three types of warm-ups needed for program safety include the musculoskeletal warm-up (called the ther-

mal warm-up), the prestretch, and the cardiorespiratory warm-up.

Thermal Warm-Up

The warm-up portion begins with a **thermal warm-up.** The thermal warm-up is aimed at the skeletal muscles on the surface of the body responsible for movement, as well as the bones that support them. It involves gentle movements, done with control, using a small range of motion that is gradually increased. This part of the warm-up is designed to bring increased bloodflow to muscles and soft tissues surrounding joints, to increase internal body temperature, and to release synovial fluid.

The thermal warm-up should last approximately three to five minutes. Major muscle groups should be used the same way they are used during the aerobic portion of the workout. All major muscle groups and joints should be used in isolation exercises and in low- to moderate-intensity exercises. Beginning slowly, using short levers and a reduced range of motion, stimulates the release of synovial fluid that lubricates joints and allows the body to gradually warm up. The later portion of the thermal warm-up can incorporate movements with a fuller range of motion, long levers, and more powerful contractions of each muscle group.

Prestretch

The **prestretch** is the next part of the warm-up. It is designed to prevent injury during a high-intensity workout. Stretching muscles that are tight from everyday living is important. Although any major muscle groups can be stretched at this point, it is important to stretch the gastrocnemius and soleus (calf), iliopsoas (hip flexors), hamstrings (back of the thigh), low back, and pectoral (chest) muscles during this portion of the workout. Stretches are usually held for 5 to 10 seconds during the prestretch. (Specific explanations of stretches are found in Chapter 4.)

The prestretch is designed to lessen the likelihood of injury during an upcoming workout. It is important to keep the body temperature at a comfortable level during stretches. If participants become chilled, muscles will contract, and injury may result if stretching continues. Keeping the upper-body limbs moving during lower-body stretches and vice versa helps to keep the muscles warm and pliable.

Cardiorespiratory Warm-Up

The **cardiorespiratory warm-up** is the last portion of the warm-up. It includes exercises with an increased range of motion and more moderate intensity. The purpose of the cardiorespiratory warm-up is to gradually overload the heart, lungs, and vascular system. It is safest and most efficient to allow those parts to adjust gradually to the increased demands. This is true for all systems in the body.

This part of the warm-up further increases oxygen demands on the heart and elevates the core temperature of the body. For example,

muscle temperature may increase as much as four degrees Fahrenheit during the entire warm-up portion. The cardiorespiratory warm-up usually lasts three to five minutes.

In order to keep body temperature up during the prestretch segment, some exercisers intersperse moves that warm and stretch a muscle group. (An example of this technique is found in Chapter 6 in the water aerobics, water-walking, and circuit-training sample workouts.)

Some aquatic exercisers feel a warm-up is unnecessary or too time consuming for their workouts. Research has shown that beginning a workout with high-intensity, vigorous exercise abnormally increases arterial blood pressure, which in turn causes heart stress. Other research has shown that warming up before a workout significantly reduces abnormal electrocardiograph readings during the vigorous phase (Cisar and Kravitz, 1989). These findings indicate that a warm-up is important to the safety of participants.

In conclusion, an effective warm-up produces many benefits; namely, it will:

—increase muscle fluidity, which improves contraction efficiency

—increase the force and rate of muscle contraction

—improve muscle elasticity and the sensitivity of the stretch reflex

—increase the flexibility of tendons, which reduces the risk of injury

—improve metabolic reactions in the muscle which promotes more efficient use of carbohydrates and fats

—increase maximal oxygen intake rate and worktime to exhaustion

The Cardiorespiratory Workout

The aerobic portion of the workout is considered the "calorie-burning" portion. The goal of this portion is to improve the cardiorespiratory system. The American College of Sports Medicine (ACSM) has made recommendations for the quantity and quality of training for developing and maintaining cardiorespiratory fitness, body composition and muscular strength, and endurance in the healthy adult (ACSM, 1990a). These guidelines address the following aspects of an aerobic exercise or **cardiorespiratory workout**:

1. *Mode*—the type of exercise necessary
2. *Duration*—the length of each workout
3. *Intensity*—how challenging the workout is for the cardiorespiratory system
4. *Frequency*—how many times a week the workout should be repeated

If a workout does not follow the guidelines for each of these four aspects, it is not considered a cardiorespiratory or aerobic workout.

Mode

The ACSM guidelines (1990a) state that in order to create the overload necessary to achieve cardiorespiratory fitness, the **mode** must be a large-muscle activity that is maintained continuously and is rhythmic in nature. This means that the large muscles in the body, such as gluteals, hamstrings, and quadriceps, must be used continuously during the aerobic portion of the workout. According to these guidelines, a workout using only upper-body movements would not qualify as aerobic. The legs also must be moving continuously for conditioning to occur.

Duration

The ACSM guidelines (1990a) regarding **duration** say that each workout should have a continuous aerobic portion, lasting between 20 and 60 minutes. Most exercise leaders consider 20 to 30 minutes the average for the aerobic portion of their classes. Classes with a longer aerobic portion usually are of lower intensity and best for students with poor fitness levels who need to improve their body composition. Long-duration, low-intensity classes are shown to be excellent "fat burners." Longer duration, however, can also lead to

overuse injuries. Students should gradually build up to longer aerobic sessions. The principle of progressive overload (discussed in Chapter 1) should be followed.

Intensity

The ACSM guidelines (1990a) regarding **intensity** state that the exercise intensity of the aerobic portion should be in a range of 50% to 85% of maximum oxygen uptake or maximum heartrate reserve, or 60% to 90% of maximum heartrate. (More in-depth information regarding heartrate and workout intensity can be found in the Appendix.) Beginning students should work at low intensity for a short duration until adaptation begins. Only people in excellent physical condition should work at an intensity in the upper portion of the range.

Frequency

The ACSM guidelines (1990a) regarding **frequency** state that a workout should occur three to five times a week in order to achieve results. Working out fewer than three times a week does not improve cardiorespiratory fitness levels. Working out more frequently than five times a week prevents the body from rebuilding and causes overuse injuries.

Cooldown

The cooldown usually lasts about five minutes and uses large, lower-intensity, rhythmic movements. The purpose of the cooldown is to aid the return of blood to the heart at a low enough intensity to allow the heart to move toward a resting level. The cooldown prevents the pooling of blood in the extremities, reduces muscle soreness, and assists in the elimination of metabolic wastes.

The cooldown in a pool is especially important because of water pressure. If a participant leaves the pool while still in the aerobic portion of the workout, dizziness can occur. When exercising at a challenging intensity, blood vessels dilate to allow for increased bloodflow during the workout. In water exercise classes, it is thought that blood vessels are pressurized by the water and do not dilate to the extent they would during land-based exercise. When exiting the pool, the lessened effect of air pressure compared to water pressure allows the blood vessels to dilate further, causing a drop in blood pressure. This can cause the participant to feel light-headed or dizzy or to actually pass out.

Toning

If **toning** or calisthenics is included in the workout it usually follows the cooldown. Trunk, upper-body, and lower-body exercises are done at pool edge or with buoyant devices that hold the participant off the bottom of the pool. (Review Chapters 4 and 6 for toning exercise ideas.)

The toning portion of the workout can last 5 to 15 minutes. Upper-body toning often is incorporated into the cooldown to conserve time. Because of the buoyancy of water, participants must be strongly encouraged to put forth the necessary effort to make water exercise effective. It is easy to cheat during water exercise because of the buoyancy and the relaxing effects of the water.

Occasionally, an instructor or student will decide to do the toning portion of a class following the thermal warm-up. There is some controversy among leaders in the field regarding the sequence of exercise classes in terms of whether the cardiorespiratory segment should precede or follow the toning work. Since no definitive research has been completed on this issue, each instructor must make a professional judgment based on the type of class he or she has and what is preferred.

Flexibility

The water aerobics class should always end with a poststretch or **flexibility** section that lasts about five minutes. If the water is warm (over 86 degrees), this section can be extended. All the major muscles used or toned during the workout should be stretched during this time. (Sample flexibility exercises are included in Chapters 4 and 6.)

The purpose of the poststretch is to provide long-term flexibility, help prevent muscle soreness, further lower the oxygen demands on the heart, and reestablish the body's equilibrium. Each muscle should be stretched beyond its normal resting length to the point of tension but not pain. If participants become chilled during the poststretch, they can get out of the pool and stretch on the deck.

Some aquatic exercise programs combine the toning and flexibility portions of the class to keep the student's body temperature comfortable and to be sure that the muscles being stretched are warm and pliable. For example, after doing toning exercises for the hamstrings, participants would stretch the hamstrings. Following toning of the abductors, students would stretch the abductors. (The sample deep-water workout in Chapter 6 has an example of mixing toning and flexibility.)

TYPES OF AQUATIC EXERCISE PROGRAMS

Water Walking

Definition

Water walking is simply striding in waist-to chest-deep water at a pace fast enough to create the overload necessary for cardiorespiratory benefits. The type of stride used should vary to ensure use of all the major muscle groups in the lower body. Most frequently, the foot action involves a heel strike, followed by rolling onto the ball of the foot and finishing with a strong push off the toes. Stride length will vary according to the participant's height, leg length, strength, and stride, as well as the water depth. The type of walking—for instance forward, sideways, or backward, with toes pointed in or out, with legs straight or bent, or on toes or heels—determines the muscles be-

DIAGRAM 2–1   Water Walking

ing used. Upper-body muscles also should be varied by using stroke, backstroke, figure eights, punching, and jogging arms. Walking sideways usually offers less resistance and can be less exertive. Arm and directional variations also can vary the intensity.

The program should follow the format for an aerobic-conditioning class.

Water Depth

Walkers usually begin in hip- to waist-depth water and walk to armpit depth before returning to shallower water. Some lucky walkers have the same depth during the entire route. Shallow water (hip to waist depth) is easier to walk in, and the pace will be faster. Deep water (midriff to shoulder depth) is more difficult to walk in and the pace will be slower.

Comparison to Land Workout

A study done at the Nicholas Institute of Sports Medicine, Lenox Hill Hospital, New York, shows that the number of calories burned during water walking increases with the depth of the water (Koszuta, 1988). The study compared dry-land walking and water walking at ankle, knee, and thigh depths and found the optimum depth to be at the thigh. Walking three miles in one hour at thigh depth was

shown to burn 460 calories. Unfortunately, this study did not include a test at waist- to chest-depth water with the increased water resistance.

A study done at the Human Performance Laboratory at the University of Georgia in Athens, Georgia, comparing water and land walking, found that water walkers got the same benefits walking 1.5 to 2 miles an hour (2.5 to 3.3 km/hr) as land walkers got at 3.5 to 8 miles an hour (5.8 to 12.4 km/hr) (Vickery, Cureton, and Langstaff, 1983). Moreover, studies done by Dr. Robert Beasley (1989) at Southern Florida State University found that oxygen uptake while walking 7 miles per hour (11.7 km/hr) on land correlated to the oxygen uptake while walking 1.8 miles per hour (2.9 km/hr) in water.

Purpose/Benefits

The major purpose of water walking is to improve cardiorespiratory endurance. Additional benefits include improved muscular endurance, flexibility (if some long strides are incorporated), and an improved body composition. Water walkers also enjoy the social benefits of group participation.

Common Errors

The two most frequent mistakes made in water walking are: (1) leaning forward while walking, and (2) using the same stride for the majority of the walk.

Proper **body alignment** is essential, and an individual should think about it during the entire walk. The head should be held in a neutral position with the chin centered, the eyes should look straight ahead (not up or down), the shoulders should be back and relaxed, the rib cage should be lifted, and the abdominals should be pulled in with the buttocks tucked under (pelvic tilt). If viewed from the side, the walker's ear, shoulder, and hip should be aligned. Walkers who lean forward probably are trying to go too fast and can compromise the low back. Maintaining good body alignment also improves abdominal and back muscle strength. Walking strides should be slow and controlled. The exception to the upright alignment is race walking in water. Race walkers lean forward slightly. Race walking is not recommended for the general population.

The second error—using the same stride for most of the workout—encourages muscle imbalance. Many walkers use their usual walking stride in the water. However, the normal walking stride contributes to overly tight hip flexors. Varying the stride allows participants to offset the natural muscle imbalance everyone has. By simply backing up, participants can ensure the use of the gluteals, hip flexors opposing muscle group. Changing to other strides allows equal use of the adductors, abductors, hamstrings, and quadriceps. Walkers should use stride variations that involve different major muscle groups to ensure **muscle balance.** Each stride should be used for an equal amount of time, unless a specific alternative plan has been set up.

Arm variations also are important. The pectoral muscles are usually tight, so using the trapezius and rhomboids against water resistance is important. Triceps should be used to offset their imbalance with the biceps. (Arm and stride variations with the muscle groups they involve are listed in Chapter 4.)

(A sample water-walking workout is in Chapter 6.)

Shallow-Water Jogging

Definition

Shallow-water jogging is much like water walking, but it is done with bounding or leaping steps. Participants who jog in the water are pushing up and partially out of the water and bouncing as they move through the water, as opposed to walkers who stride with no bounce. Like water walkers, joggers also vary their stride by moving backward, for-

DIAGRAM 2–2   Water Jogging

ward, and sideways with heels kicking up behind, knees high in front, knees out to the sides, legs straight, or jogging on toes or heels. Long, slow strides should be varied with short, fast strides. Arm movements also should be varied, using backstroke, stroke, side push, punching, and jogging arms to provide upper-body muscle balance. (Stride and arm variations are listed in Chapter 4.)

The water-jogging program should follow the format for an aerobic-conditioning class and cardiorespiratory warm-up, followed by the aerobic portion, the cooldown, toning, and poststretch.

Water Depth

Water jogging can be stressful to joints if done in water shallower than waist level. The apparent weight loss of 90% in shoulder-depth water is reduced to about 50% at waist depth. The impact of bare feet on a concrete or tile pool bottom at this depth can cause stress fractures and other overuse injuries. Midriff to shoulder depth seems to work best for shallow-water joggers. Some joggers wear buoyant belts and jog into the deeper end of the pool (5 to 12 feet) before returning to the shallow end. (For more information on deep-water jogging, see the Deep-Water Exercise section, later in this chapter.)

Most shallow-water joggers prefer to keep their arms in the water to increase the resistance for upper-body toning, endurance, and workout intensity. Using arms out of the water and overhead can destabilize the body as it moves through the water, causing alignment concerns.

Comparison to Land Workout

A study was done comparing land-running times to water-running times in an attempt to find equivalents in distance for energy expended (Osinski, 1989). This study found that an individual can run one-quarter mile in the water in the same amount of time it takes to run one mile on land. If participants are looking for a water-jogging pace guideline, this study may be beneficial.

Purpose/Benefits

The purpose of water jogging is to improve cardiorespiratory endurance and achieve all the benefits associated with it—muscular endurance, flexibility (if long strides are used), and improved body composition.

Common Errors

Water joggers make three common mistakes: (1) jogging on the toes, (2) using the same stride for the bulk of the workout, and (3) leaning forward. On land, jogging is a heel-strike sport with the heel usually landing first. In the water, jogging often is done with the forefoot landing first. Too often, the participant never follows through to bring the rest of the foot down. Jogging on the toes can lead to general muscle soreness (torn tissue), tightness and shortness in the calf muscle, shin splints (a pain in the front of the shin), and if done in water that is too shallow, stress fractures (broken bones in the foot) or other overuse injuries. The jogger should always press the heel down to the pool bottom before pushing off again.

The second mistake—using the same stride for the major part of the workout—leads to severe muscle imbalance and injury. Many joggers use their usual jogging stride in the water. However, the normal jogging stride contributes to overly tight hip flexors. Varying the stride allows participants to offset the natural muscle imbalance everyone has. By simply backing up, participants ensure use of the gluteals, the hip flexors' opposing muscle group. Changing to other strides allows equal use of the adductors, abductors, hamstrings, and quadriceps. Joggers should use stride variations that involve different major muscle groups to ensure muscle balance. Each stride should be used for an equal amount of time, unless a specific alternative plan has been set up.

Arm variations also are important. The pectoral muscles are usually tight, so using the trapezius and rhomboids against the water resistance is important. Triceps should be used to offset their imbalance with the biceps. (Arm and stride variations with the muscle groups they involve are listed in Chapter 4.)

The third problem—leaning forward while jogging forward through the water—is often a sign of trying to move too fast, which compromises the low back. Maintaining good body alignment also improves abdominal and back-muscle strength.

Proper body alignment is essential and should be thought of during the entire workout. The head should be held in a neutral position with the chin centered, the eyes should look straight ahead (not up or down), the shoulders should be back and relaxed, the rib cage should be lifted, and the abdominals pulled in with the buttocks tucked under slightly (a partial pelvic tilt). If viewed from the side, the jogger's ear, shoulder, and hip should be aligned. Joggers who lean forward probably are trying to go too fast and can compromise the low back. Most jogging strides should be slow and controlled.

The exception to the upright alignment is race jogging in the water. Race joggers lean forward slightly. Race jogging is not recommended for the general population.

Studies have concluded that the effects of water resistance and buoyancy make high levels of energy expenditure possible with relatively little movement and strain on lower-extremity joints (Evans, et al., 1978). This suggests that water jogging may be a valuable alternate mode of conditioning for developing and maintaining work capacity and cardiovascular fitness.

A study was done comparing land-running times to water-running times in an attempt to find equivalents in distance for energy expended. This study found that an individual can run one-quarter mile in the water in the same amount of time it takes to run one mile on land (Osinski, 1989). If participants are looking for a water-jogging pace guideline, this study may be beneficial.

(A sample water-jogging program is included in Chapter 6.)

Water Aerobics

Definition

Water aerobics includes a wide variety of dance and calisthenic moves performed in water. Water aerobics range from a very basic program, with extensive repetitions of kicks, jogs, and kneelifts, to a highly choreographed program, combining intricate dance and calisthenic moves.

The program should follow the format for an aerobic-conditioning class.

Water Depth

Midriff to armpit depth seems to be ideal for water aerobics. Participants experience enough buoyancy to benefit from the lessened impact, and the arms are partially immersed for upper-body toning benefits. Most participants are able to control moves at this depth. Shallower water may lead to stress fractures

DIAGRAM 2–3   Water Aerobics

and other overuse injuries. The lessened buoyancy in shallower water increases impact and the likelihood of injury. Because arms are not immersed deep enough in shallow water, it does not afford the chance for complete upper-body toning. Deeper water provides more buoyancy, but it does not allow the exerciser to fully control exercise movements. Lack of control leads to injury.

Comparison to Land Workout

Water aerobics, if done correctly, can be safer than land-based aerobics programs because of the lessened impact. Water aerobics also promotes more muscular endurance and tone because of the water's resistance, and it allows participants to remain comfortably cool during the workout.

Purpose/Benefits

The main purpose of water aerobics is to improve cardiovascular conditioning. Weight loss usually is anticipated because of the increase in oxygen consumption. Water aerobics also increases flexibility if full-range-of-motion moves are incorporated, and it enhances muscular endurance and leaner body composition.

Common Errors

Water aerobics done in shallow water (hip to waist) can cause overuse injuries and possibly heat stress syndromes. When working out in shallow water, the participant should wear well-cushioned shoes and eliminate most of the bouncing from the program. To provide a safe, muscle-balanced workout, the program should incorporate a mixture of slow, full-range-of-motion moves and faster moves. All major muscle groups should be used. Fast, ballistic moves can cause injury and should be eliminated from the program. A general rule to test the safety of the speed of the move is control—if the move is controlled and the rest of the body is stable and aligned, the speed usually is safe.

Water Toning

Definition

Water-toning programs are created specifically to improve muscular endurance. Students work a specific muscle group with one move for 15 to 60 repetitions and then move to another muscle group. Upper-body and lower-body exercises usually are alternated, with middle-body or trunk (obliques and abdominals) exercises interspersed throughout. Students usually stand at the pool edge or are supported by buoyant devices during the class.

Format

Water-toning participants must remember to include the thermal warm-up, prestretch, and poststretch portions of the program. (Review the warm-up section earlier in this chapter for the content of each portion of the program.) Muscles and joints must be prepared for the work they do during the workout.

The format for a water-toning program should begin with the thermal warm-up and prestretch, which should last at least five minutes. If participants are not feeling warmed up

DIAGRAM 2–4   Water Toning

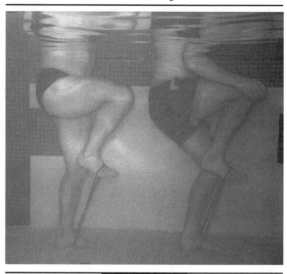

at that point, the warm-up should continue until they feel comfortable.

The toning portion of the class should follow the prestretch and can last from 15 to 40 minutes. Intensity in toning or endurance programs is determined by the amount of resistance used. Duration refers to the number of **repetitions** (reps) of each move performed within a time period and the number of times each group of reps is performed (**sets**). In general, toning or muscle-endurance training requires an overload in the number of reps. According to the rule of specificity, when designing a program for endurance development, low resistance and high reps should be used for maximum effectiveness. According to the principle of progressive overload, the instructor must progressively increase the overload on the muscle as it adapts to each new load. Frequency refers to the number of times an activity is repeated in a week.

A three- to five-minute cooldown with low-intensity, fluid, walking-level movements, followed by a poststretch of at least five minutes finishes the workout. Stretches during the prestretch only need to be held 10 seconds. Poststretches should be held 30 seconds.

Equipment

Most water-toning classes encourage students to use upper- and lower-body equipment after adapting to water exercises without equipment. Webbed gloves (by Sprint/Rothhammer or Hydro-Fit), paddles (by Sprint/Rothhammer), frisbees, buoyant bells (Nuvo Sport, Inc. Spa Bells, B-Wise fitness bars, J & B Foam), Dynabands, SPRI tubing and bands, the Aquarius Water Workout Station, small buoyant balls, and wrist weights all can be used to work the upper body. Balls, kickboards, buoyant bells, Aquarius, and resistant devices, like Spa Bells and Hydro-Tone, all can be used for middle-body work. Buoyant, weighted, and resistant ankle cuffs or boots can be worn to work the lower body. (More information regarding shoes is provided on page 45.) Stretchy exercise bands also can be used for lower-body toning.

Comparison to Land Workout

Toning in water produces quicker results than toning on land because of the water's resistance. Many of the same exercises used in land-based toning classes are used in a vertical position in the water. Unlike land-based programs, water toning participants may become chilled in the water. Using more muscular force during each exercise helps keep the body temperature in a comfortable range. Increased muscular force keeps the students from cheating or doing the move without power, and, therefore, ensures better results.

Purpose/Benefits

The benefits of water toning are increased muscular endurance and muscle mass. Increased muscle mass has a direct effect on improving body composition. If full range of motion is used, flexibility also is enhanced.

Common Errors

All the exercises must be controlled and done correctly. A general rule to test the safety of a move's speed is control—if the move is controlled and the rest of the body is stable and aligned, the speed usually is safe.

It is not a good idea to "go for the burn" during this type of exercise. Many water toners experience the burn when they begin a program. After a few weeks, as the body adapts, the burn occurs less frequently. The burn is a sign of built up **lactic acid.** The exerciser should stop a move that is causing the burn and jog in the water for 20 to 40 seconds until the muscle gets the oxygen it needs and the sensation dissipates.

Strength Training

Definition

Strength training in the water is a program aimed specifically at body building. Actual weight-lifting moves, such as squats, bicep curls, knee extensions, and elbow presses, are done in the pool during this workout. In order to attain muscular balance and reduce the risk of injuries, all major muscle groups should be strengthened during a workout, including quadriceps, hamstrings, low back, abdominals,

DIAGRAM 2–5   Strength Training

chest, upper back, shoulders, biceps, and triceps. Working all major muscle groups is important for a comprehensive and safe workout. Training just some of the muscles produces less significant results, encourages muscle imbalance, and may cause muscle injuries.

Format

A strength-training program begins with a thermal warm-up and prestretch. Since this is not a cardiorespiratory workout, no cardiorespiratory warm-up is necessary. The strength-training moves immediately follow the prestretch. Each muscle group that is strengthened during the workout must be stretched again later. This final flexibility stage can be done either at the end of the workout or after the last set in which the muscle group is used.

Use Slow and Controlled Moves with a Minimum of Momentum. It is important to perform the strength-training moves in a slow and controlled manner. Fast movements place too much stress on the muscles, connective tissues, and joints. Fast-strength training is less effective and more dangerous than slow-strength training. Participants can work with more resistance if they move quickly through the movements, but it is momentum, not muscles, doing the work. Slow training uses more muscle tension, more muscle force, and more muscle recruitment and is safer and more effective.

Full Muscle Extension to Complete Muscle Contraction. Full-range-of-motion movements should be used in strength training. This not only ensures a full **muscle contraction** but also allows the opposing muscle to stretch. Using a short range of motion has limited value on the muscle being strengthened and may lead to reduced joint mobility. To test for full range of motion in a joint, contract the muscle and move the joint without resistive equipment. When equipment is added, the joint should be able to move to full flexion and stop just short of full extension.

Systematic, Gradual Progression. The principle of progressive overload is extremely important in strength training. Resistance and reps should be gradually increased. The training stimulus must gradually overload in order to allow muscles, bones, connective tissues, and joints to adapt without injury. More demanding workouts require more recovery time.

Equipment

Some unconditioned people can do strength training in water without equipment. Highly conditioned athletes require some type of resistance equipment.

Hydro-Tone is a type of resistant equipment used for upper-, middle-, and lower-body exercises. Aquarius Water Workout Station also is used with success. Participants should never hold their breath while using resistance equipment. Exhale during the exertive lift or press, and inhale during the return or rest portion. The equipment should be gripped easily, because a clenched grip can increase blood pressure.

Almost all strength training in the water is done with equipment, based on the principle of resistance. Buoyant equipment does not work well because only one muscle of each muscle pair strengthens from the buoyancy offered. Weighted equipment approved for use in the water is not heavy enough to create the overload needed to achieve strength benefits. (For more information, contact the Aquatic Exercise Association, page 121.)

Purpose/Benefits

The main benefit of strength training is increased muscular strength and muscle mass. Increased muscle mass, which occurs when muscle protein increases and muscle fat decreases, has a direct effect on improving body composition. Muscular endurance also improves. Strength training also improves muscular balance and neuromuscular action and increases the structural integrity of muscles, connective tissues, and bones as it builds strength and density. Moderate levels of strength training also reduce the likelihood of injury. Sports enthusiasts find a strong relationship between gain in strength and gain in speed for sports involving running, cycling, and swimming.

After age 20, without strength training a body loses approximately one pound of muscle every two years. That means at age 40 someone who weighed 150 pounds at age 20 and who did no strength training will have replaced 10 pounds of muscle with 10 pounds of fat. Moreover, for every pound of muscle lost, the metabolic rate goes down about 50 calories a day. For every pound of muscle gained, the metabolic rate goes up about 50 calories a day. Strength training is necessary to keep a youthful fat-to-lean ratio in body composition.

Many exercisers believe they will build big muscles if they strength train. That is not true. Few men and fewer women have the genetic background to build big muscles. Those who have the genes to build large muscles must work long and hard to achieve them.

Strength training is particularly important for women because it staves off osteoporosis, a potentially crippling condition caused by loss of bone mineral.

Common Errors

Injuries common to weight lifters can occur in water if students begin with too much resistance, or too large a range of motion, or if they move too fast. All exercises must be controlled and done correctly. A general rule to check the safety of the move's speed is control—if the move is controlled and the rest of the body is stable and aligned, the speed usually is safe. Correct form is vital. When muscles are too fatigued to maintain correct form, the exercise should be stopped.

Without actual weight in the water, strength trainers may slow down as they tire and, in effect, reduce the weight with which they are training. The participant must be continually conscious of supplying maximum effort. Some students enjoy working with a metronome or music at a specified number of beats per minute to keep them from slowing down.

Participants should maintain the natural curve of the spine and keep feet parallel, knees soft, abdominals contracted, chest open, shoulders down and slightly back, and the back of the neck open. Instructors and students alike will be able to watch for postural imbalances by using these hints for good form. Hyperextension of the lumbar area of the spine, hip flexors, knees, and elbows should be avoided.

Guidelines

In early 1990, the ACSM set specific guidelines for resistance training programs (ACSM, 1990a). The ACSM **resistance guidelines** state that the frequency should be at least two times a week. This is considered a minimum standard and should be increased as conditioning occurs. It generally takes 48 hours for the body to repair and rebuild itself to a greater level of strength after a strength-training workout. Workouts, therefore, should be equally spaced throughout the week. Taking too little time between workouts can result in counterproductive workouts.

The ACSM duration guidelines recommend a minimum of 8 to 10 different exercises during the workout. Each exercise should be performed at least 8 to 12 times (reps). This would make up one set. While one set is the minimum considered for training to occur, more conditioned students should do multiple sets. Most muscles should be adequately stressed with 60 to 90 seconds of continuous contraction against a heavy resistance. That usually converts to 8 to 12 reps.

The guidelines also state, "Resistance strength training of a moderate intensity, sufficient to develop and maintain muscle mass, should be an integral part of an adult fitness program" (ACSM, 1990a). This strong recommendation by the ACSM points to the benefits of strength training for all adults. The latest studies also show that moderate-intensity strength training is excellent for the older adult (Strovas, 1990).

The intensity for most programs is 70% to 80% of the maximum resistance a participant can move. A general rule is that the resistance is too great if a student cannot repeat the exercise at least 8 times in a row. There is not enough resistance if the student can repeat the exercise more than 12 times.

Flexibility Training

Definition

Flexibility-training participants stretch different muscle groups to improve their long-term flexibility. Flexibility often is an ignored component of fitness.

If a muscle is only trained to contract, it loses its ability to stretch as far as it should, resulting in permanently shortened muscles. Most aquatic-fitness programs, such as ton-

DIAGRAM 2–6   Flexibility Training

ing, aerobics, and weight training, concentrate only on training the muscles to contract. Each aquatics program should include a flexibility segment.

Participants often are confused between the terms *muscle* and *joint* when attempting to understand how a flexibility class works. Muscles are *elastic,* which means they can stretch and have the ability to return to their normal position. Tight muscles, either from daily activities or from overuse in an exercise class, shorten the range of motion in the joints they move. Increased range of motion in all joints is the goal of a flexibility class. The goal is achieved by stretching the muscles that move the joints. The joint is not stretched, the muscle is. The stretched muscle, in turn, increases flexibility and, therefore, range of motion in the joint.

Muscles that are tight from daily activities need special attention during a flexibility program. Most people are round shouldered and need to stretch the pectorals. Tight hip flexors and gastrocnemius also need special attention during the program.

Format

During a flexibility-training class, students warm up a muscle group and then move to a 30- to 60-second stretch of that muscle group. For example, students may do knee extensions for 30 to 60 seconds followed by a 30- to 60-second stretch of the quadriceps. Hamstrings with knee flexion can be worked next and then stretched. Intensity is determined by overload or the amount of lengthening of the muscle beyond its resting length. The duration is determined by the type of stretching being done, how long each stretch is done, and how often each stretch is used. A frequency of three times per week is recommended for flexibility training. Care must be taken in flexibility training not to overload in ways that are harmful to the body. Muscles, like taffy, are more pliable when they are warm. Muscle temperature is greatly affected by water temperature. If muscles are warmed before stretching, safer stretching will occur.

Only static, never ballistic, stretches should be used. Fast, jerky, bouncing (**ballistic**) stretches can cause injury to tendons and microscopic tears to muscle tissue. Muscles are protected by a stretch-reflex mechanism. When a stretch is begun, a nerve reflex sends a message to contract through the brain to the muscle fibers. If a ballistic stretch is used, muscles will contract when the next bounce occurs. Attempting to stretch a contracted muscle can cause injury.

Static stretches also trigger the **stretch-reflex** mechanism to respond, but the static stretch overcomes the mechanism and allows flexibility to occur. The muscle fibers contract at the beginning of a stretch, but if the stretch is held at that point (and not pushed further), the nerve sends a signal through the brain to relax the muscle fibers again. When that occurs, the stretch can be taken a little further before the stretch-reflex responds again. Using the stretch-reflex concept in the program helps increase flexibility. Participants should move to the point of mild tension and then relax while holding the stretch in that position. After about 10 to 15 seconds, they can increase the stretch by a fraction of an inch until they feel mild tension again and then relax as they hold the stretch in that position. If the tension does not decrease, the participant should ease off the stretch and hold it at that point.

Water Depth

Average pool depth for the flexibility class is midriff level. Students should immerse problem joints (stiff joints, areas recovering from injury or surgery, and hot joints) during the warming and stretching segments. Flexibility classes also can be done in the deep end of the pool if students wear buoyant belts. Flexibility programs usually are offered in water over 86 degrees.

Comparison to Land Workout

Flexibility programs in the water work well because of the lessened effect of gravity on the joints. Exercisers are able to stretch further without undue tension. Unlike land-based flexibility exercises, almost all water-stretching exercises are done in a vertical position. Although fewer stretch positions can be used for each muscle group, those used are extremely effective.

Purpose/Benefits

The purpose of flexibility training is to increase the range of motion in each joint by elongating the muscles that move the joint. Depending on the intensity of the warm-up before stretching, the program also could increase muscular endurance and body composition.

Tight muscles can hamper joints from moving in a full range of motion. They also can pull the body out of proper alignment. A well-rounded stretching plan helps prevent muscle imbalance, and increased flexibility promotes a full range of motion.

Common Errors

The two most frequent mistakes in water-flexibility classes are (1) stretching cold muscles, and (2) stretching too far. When concentrating on flexibility, many students ignore or minimize warming a muscle before stretching it. If that happens, injury may occur. Cold muscles should not be stretched. Warming the muscle brings blood and oxygen to it, making it pliable. Warming also allows synovial fluid to lubricate the joint that moves the muscles. This allows a more comfortable, larger range of motion stretch.

Too often, students feel they should stretch until it hurts. The phrase most frequently used to describe a proper stretch is *move to the point of tension, never pain*. If performed correctly, a stretch elongates a muscle to a greater length than its resting length. Students should feel the stretch but never feel uncomfortable. Overall flexibility improves with proper stretching.

Aqua-Power Aerobics

Definition

Aqua-power aerobics is a program that combines cardiorespiratory conditioning (aerobics), strength training, and muscle toning in the aerobic portion of the workout.

Format

The class follows the usual aerobic format of thermal warm-up, prestretch, cardiovascular warm-up, aerobics, and cooldown, but it eliminates the toning portion before the final

DIAGRAM 2–7   Aqua Power

flexibility segment. Exercises are used that strengthen muscles against the water's resistance while elevating the demand for oxygen. Many low-impact-type moves—such as lunges, squats, and sidekicks—can be used. Moves are done slowly and with control and power. Explosive muscle force is used in each move. More reps are used if muscle toning is desired with the aerobics. Fewer reps and more resistance are used for aerobics with strength training.

Equipment

Equipment often is used after students have mastered the moves and have adapted to the exercise level without equipment. Webbed gloves (by Hydro-Fit or Sprint/Rothhammer), wrist and ankle weights, Dynabands, SPRI exercise bands and tubing, buoyant ankle and wrist cuffs (by Hydro-Fit or Sprint/Rothhammer), and any lightly resistant product can be used. Advanced aqua-power aerobics students may want to experiment with more highly resistant and buoyant equipment, such as Nuvo Sport Spa Bells, B-Wise Fitness Bars, or Hydro-Tone. (See the Appendix for more information about equipment.)

Water Depth

Beginning classes use waist-depth water to make students feel more comfortable and successful in performing power moves. In shallow water, exercisers concentrate better on leg movement and proper technique. More advanced classes usually use deeper water (chest depth) for added effectiveness.

Purpose/Benefits

The purpose of aqua-power aerobics is to increase cardiorespiratory fitness, muscular endurance and muscular strength, and to improve body composition.

Flexibility also can be enhanced through the flexibility segment at the end of the class.

Common Errors

The most difficult tasks in an aqua-power class are teaching correct technique to students and helping them understand that slow moves can be aerobic. Some instructors have students review power moves on the deck to demonstrate technique. In water, students need to maintain a proper alignment and learn to use explosive muscle force in the correct portion of the move.

Sport-Specific and Sports-Conditioning Workouts

Definition

Sport-specific workouts are aerobic workouts that are designed to assist sports enthusiasts in developing the muscle strength and flexibility, skills, agility, balance, and coordination needed in their sport.

Format

The format of the workout begins with the traditional thermal warm-up, stretch, and cardiorespiratory warm-up. Power, balance, coordination, and sports skills and patterns are worked on during the aerobic portion. The concept of interval training can be used during the aerobic portion of the workout. Strength conditioning or muscle endurance can be worked on following the cooldown. Flexibility for specific needs follows the strength-conditioning or muscular endurance portion.

Sport-specific conditioning can be done for enthusiasts in most sports, including baseball, javelin, biking, running, downhill skiing, tennis, weight lifting, football, soccer, cross-country skiing, and track and field. Enthusiasts from different sports can take part in the same aqua aerobics class if different stations are used and time is spent interviewing participants before they enroll. The entire class would stay together during the warm-up and for some of the agility, coordination, and speed drills in the aerobic portion of the class. That

DIAGRAM 2–8   Sport Specific and Sports Conditioning

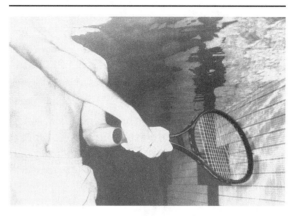

Sport Specific

Sports Conditioning

ensures muscle balance in the workout. Participants then would move around the pool from station to station, each of which is designed to assist athletes in developing the skills and strength needed in their particular sports. If equipment is needed, it would be at pool edge at the station.

Following the specific exercises, the class would come together again for the cooldown, upper- and lower-body strength exercises (once again for muscle balance), and the flexibility segment. If sport-specific flexibility is necessary, it would follow the group flexibility segment and be done at stations.

If the goal is to improve in a particular sport, the instructor and student need to look at the requirements of that sport:

— What muscles need to be especially strong? Which need to be particularly flexible?
— Is speed important? If it is, is it speed moving forward, backward, or laterally? Is it speed of limb movement?
— What kinds of agility and coordination are required?
— What specific skills are needed?

Note where the student feels aches, pains, and stiffness after the sport so those areas can be conditioned against injury.

Equipment

The actual equipment that is used in the sport can be used in the pool. Baseball bats, golf clubs, and tennis racquets are seen in pools during sport-specific workouts. It is important to note that the equipment, like any aquatic equipment, should always be used with control and safety in mind. Aquatic equipment like Hydro-Fit, Hydro-Tone, Aquarius, B-Wise Fitness Bars, Nuvo Sport Spa Bells and SPRI tubing and Dynabands are used in sport-specific training to help stretch, strengthen, and tone specific muscles. It is also used to simulate moves in the sport. (See the Appendix for information on equipment.)

Comparison to Land Workout

Sports-conditioning and -training workouts in water closely compare to those on land. Exercisers can challenge the muscles they use in their sport more easily with water resistance. They can increase muscular strength, agility, balance, and aerobic conditioning without the stress of land-based sports drills.

Purpose/Benefits

The purpose of sport-specific training can be as varied as the participant's needs. Most programs have aerobic or cardiorespiratory and body composition improvements as their main goals. Improved muscular endurance, flexibility, and muscular strength usually are secondary goals.

Common Errors

The most common mistake made in sport-specific training is working only on strengthening those muscles needed during the sport. A goal in this type of program should be creating muscle balance in the athlete. All major muscle groups should be used. Determine the major muscle groups used in the sport and develop agonists and antagonists equally.

Flexibility too often is ignored, even though its importance in injury prevention is well documented. All major muscles should be stretched, with special attention given to those muscles that need to stretch during the sport.

Sport-specific classes usually are designed for fit or conditioned participants who want to increase their abilities in their chosen sports. They generally are not classes for beginners or unconditioned individuals.

Bench or Step Aerobics
Definition

Bench aerobics or step workouts are aerobic workouts that mimic the Harvard Step Test for cardiorespiratory fitness. (During the test, participants step up and down on a bench for three minutes and then check working and recovery heartrates.) Rather than have participants step up and down on a bench for just three minutes, the step workout makes up the entire aerobic portion of the class. Participants

DIAGRAM 2–9   Bench Aerobics

use stairs in the pool or weighted benches taken into the pool to step up and down in a rhythmic fashion. Moving the body vertically against gravity creates an intense aerobic workout that focuses on the lower body. It is a high-intensity, low-impact workout.

Format

The class begins with the traditional thermal warm-up, stretch, and cardiorespiratory warm-up. The aerobic segment usually lasts 20 to 40 minutes and is made up exclusively of stepping up and down in a variety of patterns. Traditional cooldown and flexibility segments follow the aerobic portion. The flexibility segment should give special attention to the quadriceps, gluteals, and hamstrings, because they do the bulk of the stepping work. A strength or

toning portion can be included between the cooldown and flexibility portions, but it normally is excluded because of the toning achieved during the aerobics portion. Depending on water depth, an upper-body strength or toning portion can be included during the cooldown. If the pool is shallow, additional upper-body toning against the water's resistance is needed.

Equipment

A bench or step such as the Aqua Step or Aerobic Workbench is the only equipment needed for the program. Benches used in the pool usually are weighted with diving weights to hold them in position. Benches should be stable to ensure safety. The bench can vary from two to twelve inches in height. Four- to eight-inch benches usually are recommended, because they will accommodate most fitness levels. The step should not flex the knee beyond 90 degrees.

Water Depth

Average water depth for step training should be midriff level. Step training offers a higher level of intensity because the body pushes more water out of the way when stepping out. If a student feels too buoyant or does not have control of the steps, the water level should be lowered.

Comparison to Land Workout

Studies done by Drs. Lorna and Peter Francis at San Diego State University show that land-based step training offers the energy expenditure of running at a seven-minute-per-mile pace with the amount of impact shock to the lower limbs produced by walking (Aldridge, 1990). The impact in water is lessened even more. Bench aerobics on land offers the resistance of gravity and body weight when stepping up. In water, the body works against the resistance of body weight, some gravity, and some water resistance. When stepping down in the water, the body needs to work against water resistance and buoyancy.

Music

Music used during the workout helps keep students on a cadence that challenges them. The tempo used for step classes is usually 100 to 110 beats per minute. Strom-Berg Productions is the only music service that has created a tape specific for aquatic step-training.

Purpose/Benefits

Step-training benefits include cardiorespiratory improvement, increased muscular endurance, and improved body composition. Flexibility gains can be made if a flexibility portion is included at the end of the workout. Muscular strength can improve if additional equipment is used. Balance and coordination also will improve.

Step training is popular among conditioned men and women. Women often appreciate the additional work for the thighs and buttocks, and both women and men enjoy the challenge of this athletic workout.

Common Errors

Students need constant encouragement and advice to help them maintain proper alignment and correct technique. They should step to the center of the platform, keep shoulders back, chest up, buttocks tucked under hips, and knees soft. The entire sole of the foot should make contact with the bench when stepping up. When stepping down, the ball of the foot touches first and then the heel. The knees should not lock on the step up or on the step down. The body always should be carried tall with shoulders centered over the hips. Leaning backward or forward during any portion of the step training is unnecessary and could cause muscle imbalance or injury. The feet should usually start and finish next to each other.

The most common mistake made in step training is using the same step pattern for the entire workout. Add variety to the workout by stepping or walking around, in front, or to the sides of the bench. This provides a better opportunity for muscle balance. Overuse of the quadriceps and hip flexors can cause knee and back injury.

Interval Training

Definition

Interval training is an exertive exercise program usually reserved for well-conditioned athletes. The program can, however, be modified for less-conditioned people. Interval train-

DIAGRAM 2–10   Interval Trailing

ing simply means a workout that combines high-intensity portions with moderate- or low-intensity segments.

During continuous aerobic training, the exercise program is organized so the workout intensity remains in the target heartrate zone during the entire workout. The intensity begins at the low end of the target zone and gradually increases to moderate and high intensity before tapering back to the low end. Interval training is unique in that it is based on short bouts of intense exercise, during which the workout intensity is at the top end of the target zone. These high-intensity bouts are separated by recovery periods, during which the workout intensity is at the low to moderate portions of the target zone. This technique trains the athlete to maintain near-maximum heartrate for a longer total time than would be possible with continuous training. This type of training uses the anaerobic metabolic pathway. The primary fuel is intramuscular glycogen.

Format

Intervals usually are done as part of the aerobics portion of a workout. The format for a cardiorespiratory workout includes a thermal warm-up, prestretch, and cardiorespiratory warm-up. The aerobics portion usually begins with three minutes of aerobics at low or moderate intensity. Approximately 75 seconds are allotted for the high-intensity interval before returning to moderate or low intensity for three more minutes. Five to seven cycles are done during the aerobics part of the program before cooling down, toning, and stretching.

A **cycle** is the combination of one low- (or moderate-) and one high-intensity set. The low- to moderate-intensity portion is usually at 60% to 75% of the target heartrate. The high-intensity part of the cycle is usually at 75% to 80% of the target heartrate zone and is designed to move at least to, and often beyond, the anaerobic threshold.

The **work-to-recovery ratio** is how long the high intensity (work) lasts in comparison to the moderate or low intensity (recovery). Most interval-training programs use a 1 to 3 or a 1.5 to 3 work-to-recovery ratio. This means 60 to 75 seconds of high intensity (anaerobic) are followed by three minutes of low to moderate intensity (aerobic) for each cycle. Some programs use a 1 to 2 ratio and others a 1 to 1 ratio. The most common is a 1 to 3 work-to-recovery ratio.

Comparison to Land Workout

Interval training can be achieved more safely and effectively in water than on land. Working against water resistance allows the exerciser to move into a high-intensity workout without the stress received in land-based interval-training programs.

Purpose/Benefits

The goal of interval training is to improve the cardiorespiratory system; thus, benefits will be seen not only in the fitness component of cardiorespiratory fitness but also in body composition because of the impact on caloric consumption. Muscular endurance also can be improved during the program; and muscular strength can be improved during the strength or toning portion of the class. Flexibility can be improved through the use of full range of motion and the final stretch.

Common Errors

Participants of interval-training classes need to be aware that while increasing the speed of the movements may elevate the heartrate and perceived exertion level, it may compromise the joints and connective tissues. Too many times, exercisers try to increase the intensity by only increasing the speed of the movements. Using equipment, increasing frontal resistance, increasing acceleration, and using long levers all can increase the workout's intensity. Moving through water also increases energy requirements.

Interval training, like all fitness programs, should work toward improving muscle balance. All major muscle groups should be worked and stretched during the workout.

Modifications can be made to the program to open participation to less-conditioned individuals. The 3-minute moderate-intensity portion can be followed by a 75-second low-intensity portion, while other participants are doing 75 seconds of high intensity. The 75-second part of the cycle can be the recovery portion for less-conditioned participants.

Deep-Water Exercise

Definition

Deep-water exercise refers to any type of water exercise program done in the diving well of the pool or in water depth above a participant's head. It is a completely nonimpact workout. With every footfall on land, the legs bear two to five times the body's weight; in deep water, the legs bear none.

Deep-water exercise usually falls into one of two categories—running or exercises. Deep-water running is simply running in deep water, using different strides. Deep-water exercises usually constitute a class that follows the format for an aerobic workout, usually including some deep-water running. Deep-water exercises can be added to any program for variety.

Format

Many people get into the pool and start running immediately, but a well thought out program takes the runners through a complete warm-up segment before beginning the run, and finishes with cooldown and flexibility segments after the run. Deep-water exercise programs should always follow the format for a safe, effective cardiorespiratory workout. (The format is reviewed at the beginning of this chapter.)

Exercises done in the shallow end can be done in deep water with one precaution—all

DIAGRAM 2–11   Deep-Water Training

movements should be bilateral. Rather than kick one leg forward, a deep-water exerciser should kick one leg forward while kicking the other back. Rather than kick one leg out to the side, the deep-water exerciser should match the movement on the other side with the other leg. In order to keep good balance and alignment in deep water, every move needs to be balanced by an opposite move.

Equipment

All participants in deep-water exercise should use flotation belts or vests. An AquaJogger, Wet Vest, Hydro-Tone, Sprint/Rothhammer and J & B Foam's belt all work to keep the exerciser afloat. Even good swimmers and floaters should wear flotation devices so they can concentrate on performing the exercises correctly, rather than on treading water.

The workout intensity can be increased by using equipment like Hydro-Fit that not only keeps the participants afloat but also increases the resistance. These kinds of equipment use the concepts of both buoyancy and resistance, rather than just buoyancy. As with all equipment designed to increase intensity, the principle of progressive overload should be followed. (See the Appendix for more information about equipment.)

Water Depth

Although most deep-water training occurs in water 8 to 12 feet deep, shallower water can be used. With the proper buoyant equipment, exercisers can do deep-water training in water three to four inches less than their heights. For example, a 5-foot, 4-inch individual can deep-water train in water five feet deep.

Comparison to Land Workout

Long-distance runners are told to put in one hundred miles a week during training. Deep-water exercise makes that obsolete. With three or four deep-water workouts a week, long-distance runners can cut their mileage up to 50%. A Clemson University runner whose personal best for the mile was 4 minutes, 18 seconds trained in the water for four weeks and was able to run a 4-minute, 3-second mile (Murphy, 1985).

Purpose/Benefits

The purpose of deep-water exercise is to improve cardiorespiratory fitness. Other benefits include improvements in body composition, flexibility, and muscular endurance. Deep-water exercise is especially suited to the well-conditioned participant but it also works well for injured, older, and obese adults who cannot tolerate any impact. Other advantages to deep-water exercise include reduced pressure on joints and bones, elimination of neuromuscu-

lar trauma, and an increased speed and endurance.

Common Errors

The most common mistake in deep-water exercise is poor alignment. Most exercisers lean forward, backward, or to the side during different exercises. Poor alignment makes the exercises easier to do but keeps from working the proper muscles. Leaning forward while running through the water makes it easier to cover more space, more quickly. Keeping the body in an upright, vertical, aligned posture creates more frontal resistance and, therefore, increases the intensity. This keeps the body in good alignment during training, causes cocontraction in the abdominal and back muscles, strengthens them, and allows the muscles that are being used to properly work, contract, and elongate.

Circuit Training

Definition

Circuit training is an aerobic workout that combines strength training and aerobic conditioning. Circuit training takes place during the aerobic portion of a cardiorespiratory workout. The program follows the format for all cardiorespiratory workouts defined earlier in this chapter. The complete warm-up (thermal, stretch, and cardio) is followed by a 20- to 40-minute circuit-training aerobic portion. Participants work one muscle group, usually with equipment, for 30 to 60 seconds, and then move to aerobics for 1 to 3 minutes. Following the aerobic interval, participants work another muscle group. This is continued until all major muscle groups have been used for 20 to 40 minutes. The cooldown follows, with the poststretch or flexibility segment at the end.

Format

Strength circuits usually are set up in stations around the edge of the pool so stu-

DIAGRAM 2–12   Circuit Training

dents can move to a different station during each strength segment. This is called the **self-guided method.** Only students who are well motivated and understand how to perform the moves at each station will achieve good results. If all the participants need more help and there is enough equipment, everyone in the class can move to the edge of the pool and do the same strength move together. This allows the instructor to give the group motivational hints, correctional cues, and information on the muscle being used. This is called the **group-travel method.** People at all fitness levels are able to participate in circuit-training programs by personally modifying the intensity level of the strength and aerobic portions of the workout.

Equipment

Many different kinds of equipment can be used during circuit training. SPRI tubing, Dynabands, buoyant devices (such as Nuvo Sport Spa Bells, J & B Foam, B-Wise Fitness Bars, Hydro-Fit, and Sprint/Rothhammer), resistant devices (such as Nuvo Sport Spa Bells and Hydro-Tone), weights, and the Aquarius Water Workout Station all help create the overload needed on the muscles during the strength circuits. The equipment should be simple to put on, and it should be left on throughout the entire workout to be sure the training intensity level is not lost. (See Appendix for more information about equipment.)

Purpose/Benefits

The goal of aquatic circuit training is to achieve both cardiorespiratory fitness and improved muscular strength. Body composition, muscular endurance, and flexibility also improve during a circuit-training program. Both strength trainers who want to add cardiorespiratory training to their workout and aerobics students who want to add some strength training to their workout benefit from circuit training. Circuits add variety to the workout and help students avoid burnout and exercise plateaus. The minor components of physical fitness (coordination, power, agility, and balance) all improve. People at all fitness levels are able to participate in circuit-training programs by personally modifying the intensity level of the strength and aerobic portions of the workout.

Since circuit training has become popular, other kinds of circuits have also been developed. Sports circuits using sports-conditioning moves at different stations can be done. Motor-skill circuits, calisthenic circuits, and interval-training circuits also can be done.

Common Errors

A common mistake made during circuit training is losing continuous movement and, therefore, aerobic training effect. Students who tire during the strength stations need to be reminded to keep moving even if they have to slow down. Students also can lose aerobic conditioning while moving to the pool edge if they do not move quickly. Picking up or putting on equipment is another time when students may stop continuous movement. If continuous movement is not stressed, the workout loses many of its benefits.

Strength-training moves should be full range of motion, slow, and controlled. All major muscles should be used during a circuit-training class. (Read the Strength Training segment, earlier in this chapter, for more information on speed of moves and muscle balance.)

Alignment is important. Students' hips, shoulders, and ears should be in a straight line if viewed from the side. Proper postural alignment helps prevent injuries in the exercise program.

The strength-training moves should be powerful, putting as much muscle as possible behind each rep. Power, not speed, should be encouraged.

Plyometric Training

Definition

Plyometrics has become popular as a training technique to improve power, speed, and jumping abilities in athletes. **Plyometric training** involves a series of jumping, bounding, and hopping moves. The program begins with the easiest type of exercise (inplace jumps) and progresses to the most demanding (bench jumps). Plyometrics is an anaerobic training program that is used by highly conditioned athletes whose sports involve power, speed, or jumping. It can be incorporated into a water aerobics class for the well conditioned. Plyometric moves work well in sport-specific-training, circuit-training, and interval-training programs.

Inplace jumps (described in Chapter 4) used in plyometrics include scissor jumps, jumping-jack jumps, and tuck jumps. Inplace jumps begin with two feet and progress to one-foot jumps.

Hops are the next progression and include skipping, hopping, and hopping up steps. Participants begin in place and gradually move forward, backward, and sideways. During these hops, the athlete jumps up with complete plantar flexion of the ankle joint.

DIAGRAM 2–13 Plyometrics

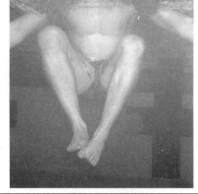

Bounding is the next progression. It involves both inplace jumps and hopping, covering as much distance as possible.

Bench jumps are the final progression. These involve jumping on and off benches that are 10 to 20 inches high (depending on the conditioning level of the participant) using tuck jumps, long jumps, and side jumps.

Format

Participants begin with about 12 reps of each jump and progress to about 20. A total of 100 jumps per workout for a beginning program and 300 jumps per workout for an advanced program is average. Maximum effort should be expended during each move. A rest period of one to two minutes between exercises is required.

Equipment

Equipment is unnecessary for beginning students but can be added as students progress. Resistant equipment, such as Hydro-Tone and Nuvo Sport Spa Bells, increases drag and enhances intensity. Other equipment, like aqua gloves by Sprint/Rothhammer and Hydro-Fit, can improve distance jumps while using upper-body muscles. (See Appendix for more information about equipment.)

Comparison to Land Workout

Plyometric training done in water allows the exerciser to work out with less incidence of injury because of water buoyancy. The exerciser is challenged more in water than on land because of water resistance.

Purpose/Benefits

The purpose of plyometric training is not to achieve aerobic conditioning but rather anaerobic conditioning. Benefits include increased aerobic capacity, increased muscular strength and endurance, and improved body composition.

Common Errors

The most common error made in classes using plyometric moves is allowing students to slow down and not use maximum effort. Participants should make an all-out effort all the time.

Relaxation Techniques

Purpose

Relaxation techniques frequently are used to augment or add variety to aquatic exercise classes. Some of the techniques discussed can be done while in the water; others need to be done on the deck. It is possible to use just portions of any of these relaxation techniques during a two- to three-minute relaxation period at the end of class.

DIAGRAM 2–14   Relaxation

Exercise participants often are unconsciously tense or tight because of stressful situations in their everyday lives. As the specific muscles that are tense or tight get tired of being continually contracted, they "give notice" by feeling sore and being stiff and aching, freezing, or going into spasm. The muscles that are habitually contracted by tension are being forced to work when no work is required. This tends to shorten these muscles, which contributes to muscular imbalance, which in turn causes aches or pains and further tightening. Relaxation techniques can assist participants in improving muscle balance.

Types

There are two basic types of relaxation techniques. Muscle-to-mind approaches use muscular contraction and release to make the entire body—including the mind—relax. Mind-to-muscle techniques use the mind and its abilities to relax the entire body, including the muscles.

Muscle-to-Mind. Breath awareness is one example of a muscle-to-mind relaxation approach. Breathing techniques are the simplest tools for promoting relaxation. Simply being aware of each inhalation and exhalation begins the relaxation approach. Participants are encouraged to feel that fresh, clean air is entering the body during the inhalation and that impurities are leaving the body during exhalation. Participants also are asked to pay attention to the time between inhalation and exhalation; some count to any number between 4 and 10 during each inhalation and exhalation.

Progressive relaxation is another muscle-to-mind relaxation technique. Participants contract specific muscles in the body and then relax them to "let go." The progression generally goes up through the body, beginning with the feet. The progression also can work down, beginning with the head. Each muscle group is contracted approximately 5 times for 10 seconds each time. The first one or two contractions are strong all-out contractions. The following two contractions use only half the tension, and the last contraction is barely strong enough to be felt.

Mind-to-Muscle. Meditation is a form of mind-to-muscle relaxation technique. It focuses one's attention on a single syllable or sound. The participant attempts to totally clear his or her mind from any interfering thoughts or distractions.

Benson's relaxation response is another mind-to-muscle technique. A Harvard cardiologist named Herbert Benson brought some of the concepts and principles of Eastern forms of meditation to the West (Riposo, 1985). His relaxation response technique is similar to meditation. The environment must be comfortable and quiet. Benson uses words, such as *one* and *relax* as the syllable or sound to be repeated. He recommends that participants have a passive attitude during meditation, allowing thoughts to come into the mind, gently pushing them back out, and refocusing on the word or sound.

Imagery or visualization is a relaxation technique frequently used by aerobics instructors. Research shows that by imagining themselves in successful situations, people can enhance their own success. This concept is used in imagery and visualization relaxation. The instructor often verbally guides the class into a relaxing environment, such as a beach or mountain retreat. The relaxing environment is then described by the instructor in more detail, while the participants relax and visualize the new setting.

Autogenic training is a form of relaxation in which the body is trained to produce sensations of heaviness and warmth. The learning process is based on techniques similar to meditation and visualization, with concentration focused on the sensations. There are six stages of application for the technique:

1. heaviness in the arms and then the legs
2. warmth in the arms and the legs
3. heartrate regulation
4. breathing-rate regulation
5. warmth in the solar plexus
6. coolness in the forehead

Instructors using imagery and visualization talk students through this type of relaxation technique, going through each of the six stages gradually.

CHOOSING AN AQUATIC FITNESS PROGRAM

Choosing a program can be confusing. Cardiorespiratory fitness and body composition change are the goals of most participants. Many want to lose weight, which can be done best by burning calories through cardiorespiratory or aerobic training. Most want to look good, which comes from having a good lean-to-fat mass ratio, or good body composition. That is achieved best through cardiorespiratory training with some strength training. Match the goal with the purpose of the class.

The instructor should be adequately trained to create an aquatic fitness program. **Instructor certification** programs are offered by the Aquatic Exercise Association.

Certification shows that the instructor has studied for and passed a training program of basic standards to teach aquatic exercise. The instructor should accept all persons in class, make modifications for special situations, and be prompt, courteous and motivating. (See page 121 for more information.)

Heartrate or perceived exertion should be checked during an aerobics class to be sure cardiorespiratory conditioning is taking place.

All classes should begin with a warm-up before getting into the actual work segment of the class. All classes should end with a cooldown and final stretch segment. All classes also should include balanced workouts in terms of muscle groups used.

Finding programs that meet specific needs can be challenging but also rewarding. Fitness goals can be met easily with the right class or mix of classes.

KEY WORDS

Warm-up	Water walking	Aqua-power aerobics
Thermal warm-up	Shallow water jogging	Sport-specific workouts
Prestretch	Water aerobics	Bench aerobics
Cardiorespiratory warm-up	Water toning	Interval training
Intensity	Repetitions	Cycle
Cardiorespiratory workout	Lactic acid	Work-to-recovery ratio
Mode	Muscle contraction	Deep-water exercise
Duration	Sets	Circuit training
Frequency	ACSM resistance guidelines	Self-guided method
Toning	Flexibility training	Group-travel method
Flexibility	Static	Plyometric training
Body alignment	Ballistic	Relaxation techniques
Muscle balance	Stretch-reflex	Instructor certification

SUMMARY

— The format of aquatic exercise programs varies depending on their goals.

— Water aerobic classes usually begin with a thermal warm-up.

— A prestretch segment after the thermal warm-up is designed to prevent injury during the workout.

— The cardiorespiratory warm-up includes moderate intensity moves and follows the prestretch.

— The aerobic portion, following the cardio-respiratory warm-up, is the "calorie-burn-ing" segment.

— The cooldown uses large, rhythmical move-ments.

— Toning or strength work usually follows the cooldown.

— The water aerobics class always should end with a poststretch or flexibility section.

— The ACSM has made recommendations re-garding the mode, duration, intensity and frequency of a quality training program.

— Water walking is simply striding in waist-to-chest-deep water.

— Shallow-water jogging is done with bound-ing or leaping steps.

— Water aerobics includes a wide variety of dance and calisthenic moves.

— Water-toning programs are created spe-cifically to improve muscular endurance.

—Strength training in water is a program aimed specifically at body building.

—Flexibility-training participants stretch different muscle groups to improve their long-term flexibility.

—Aqua-power aerobics is a program that combines cardiorespiratory conditioning, strength training, and muscle toning in the aerobic portion of the workout.

—Sport-specific workouts are aerobic workouts that are designed to assist sports enthusiasts in developing the muscle strength and flexibility, skills, agility, balance, and coordination needed in their sport.

—Bench workouts are aerobic workouts that achieve cardiorespiratory conditioning through stepping up and down on a bench.

—Interval training is an exertive exercise program usually reserved for well-conditioned athletes.

—Deep-water exercise refers to any type of water exercise program done in water depth above the participant's head.

—Circuit training is an aerobic workout that combines strength training and aerobic conditioning.

—Plyometric training is a popular training technique to improve power, speed, and jumping abilities in athletes.

—Relaxation techniques frequently are used to augment or add variety to aquatic exercise classes.

—Match the goal of the participant to the purpose of the class when choosing a fitness program.

—Be sure the instructor is qualified.

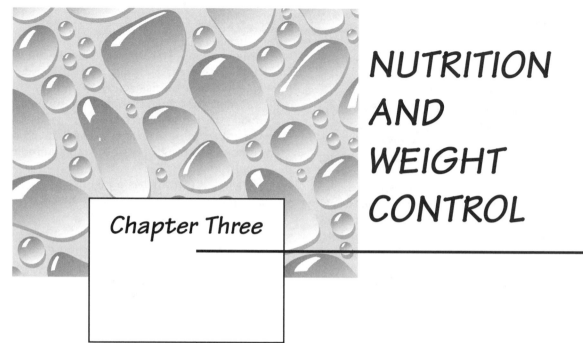

Chapter Three

NUTRITION

The most important thing a student can do to enhance his or her state of health is maintain proper **nutrition.** The body cannot function well without a proper supply of nutrients and energy. Students need to know the basics of good nutrition to ensure their diets supply the best possible balance of nutrients for good health and adequate calories to meet their energy requirements.

Water

Water is the most essential nutrient and also probably the most important in relation to physical performance. Approximately 60% of body weight is water that comes from three sources: (1) fluids we drink, (2) water in foods (lettuce and celery are over 90% water, bread is about 36%), and (3) metabolic water, which is the by-product of numerous chemical reactions in the body.

Under normal circumstances, about two quarts of water are lost each day. Water leaves the body in urine and feces, in exhaled air, and through the skin. Kidney function maintains the crucial and delicate balance of water in the body.

During exercise, water is needed to control body temperature. This is achieved through the production and evaporation of sweat through the skin. In addition to water, sweat contains *electrolytes*—the **minerals** sodium, potassium, and chloride—which are important for fluid balance and nerve and muscle function. Inadequate water intake before and during exercise adversely affects athletic performance and heat tolerance, possibly leading to heat cramps, heat exhaustion, and heatstroke.

Cardiovascular performance also can be impaired. Fluid depletion lowers blood volume, leading to decreased stroke volume and a corresponding increase in heartrate at the same workload. As temperature and humidity increase, so does the need for water.

Drinking water is the safest way to replace lost sweat. It is important to be aware that during heavy exercise, thirst is not a good indicator of the need for water. It is a good practice to drink water before, during, and after exercise.

Guidelines for Good Nutrition

In 1979, the U.S. Food and Drug Administration developed four broad classifications of foods, based on certain key **nutrients** (Riposo, 1990). The groups include fruits and vegetables, grain products, milk and milk products, and meats and meat substitutes. While recommendations for the number of servings per day from each group vary, based on age and growth development, a recommended average diet includes the following:

- Fruits and vegetables, 4 servings daily
- Grain products (breads and cereals), 4 servings daily
- Milk and milk products, 2 servings daily
- Meats and meat substitutes, 2 servings daily

The recommended servings from the basic four food groups furnish approximately 1,200 to 1,500 calories per day and adequate amounts of essential nutrients, provided a variety of foods are selected.

In 1977, the Senate Agricultural Subcommittee on Nutrition set the following dietary guidelines to improve Americans' health and quality of life:

1. Avoid becoming overweight by consuming only as much energy (**calories**) as can be expended. If overweight, decrease energy intake, and increase energy expenditure.
2. Eat enough complex **carbohydrates** and naturally occurring sugars to account for about 40% of energy intake. Do this by eating fresh fruits, vegetables, whole grains, and products made with stoneground flour. Restrict the intake of refined sugars and fruits that contain sucrose, corn sugar, and corn syrup.
3. Limit overall fat consumption to approximately 30% of your energy intake. Restrict consumption of saturated fats by choosing meats, poultry, fish, and dairy products that are low in saturated fat. Restrict consumption of saturated fats to about 10% of the total energy intake, with polyunsaturated fats accounting for 20%.
4. Maintain **cholesterol** consumption at about 300 mg per day by controlling the amount of milk products, eggs, and butter fat consumed.
5. Limit intake of sodium to less than 5 grams per day by controlling consumption of salt and processed foods.
6. Reduce consumption of artificial colorings, artificial flavorings, thickeners, preservatives, and other food additives. (Riposo, 1985)

In 1979, the Department of Agriculture and the Department of Health and Human Services published "Nutrition and Your Health, Dietary Guidelines for Americans," which is the source of the following recommendations:

1. Eat a variety of foods daily, including selections of fruits; vegetables; whole-grain and enriched breads, cereals, and grain products; milk, cheese, and yogurt; meats, poultry, fish, and eggs; and legumes (dry peas and beans).
2. Maintain acceptable body weight by losing any excess and improving eating habits. To lose weight, increase physical activity, eat less fat and fatty foods, eat less sugar and sweets, and avoid too much alcohol. To improve eating habits, eat slowly, prepare smaller portions, and avoid seconds.
3. Avoid too much fat, saturated fat, and cholesterol. Choose lean meat, fish, poultry, dry beans, and peas as **protein**

sources. Moderate consumption of eggs and organ meats (liver). Limit intake of butter, cream, hydrogenated margarines, shortenings, coconut oil, and foods made from such products. Trim excess fat off meats. Broil, bake, or boil rather than fry. Read labels carefully to determine both amounts and types of fat contained in foods.

4. Eat foods with adequate *starch* and *fiber*: Substitute starches for fats and sugars, and select foods that are good sources of fiber and starch, such as whole-grain breads and cereals, fruits and vegetables, beans, peas, and nuts.

5. Avoid too much sugar. Use less of all sugars, including white sugar, brown sugar, raw sugar, honey, and syrup. Eat less food containing these sugars, such as candy, soft drinks, ice cream, cake, and cookies. Select fresh fruits or canned fruits without sugar or in light syrup rather than heavy syrup. Read food labels for clues on sugar content. If the ingredients *sucrose, glucose, maltose, dextrose, lactose, fructose,* or *syrups* appear first, the product contains a large amount of sugar. And remember: How *often* you eat sugar is as important as how *much* sugar you eat.

6. Avoid too much **sodium.** Learn to enjoy the unsalted flavors of foods. Cook with only small amounts of added salt. Add little or no salt to foods at the table. Limit intake of salty foods, such as potato chips, pretzels, salted nuts, popcorn, condiments (soy sauce, steak sauce, garlic salt), cheese, pickled foods, and cured meats. Read food labels carefully to determine amounts of sodium in processed foods and snack items.

7. If you drink alcohol, do so in moderation. Refrain from sustained or heavy drinking (more than two drinks per day).

WEIGHT CONTROL

When considering the issues of body weight and body fat, it is useful to think of the body as being composed of two distinct parts: (1) lean body mass, and (2) fat body mass. The *lean body mass* is the fat-free component, which consists of water, electrolytes, minerals, glycogen stores, muscle tissue, internal organs, and bones.

Fat body mass, or **body fat,** is composed of two parts: essential fat and storage fat. *Essential fat* is necessary for normal physiological functioning and nerve conduction. It makes up approximately 3% to 7% of total body weight in men and about 15% in women. *Storage fat,* which is also called *depot fat,* constitutes anywhere from a few percent of total body weight on a lean individual to 40% to 50% of body weight on an obese person. For most people, concerns about being overweight actually are concerns about being overfat. Body-fat standards for men indicate that lean is 5% to 10%, ideal is 18%, and obese is 20% and over. Body-fat standards for women show lean as 10% to 20%, ideal as 22%, and obese as 30% and over.

Fads and Fallacies

Current social standards call for the slim-and-fit look. The weight-control industry has cashed in on this ideal; it is bigger than ever, with annual sales over $220 million. Unfortunately, some weight-control regimens and products make exaggerated claims and are grossly misleading. Whatever weight loss they produce usually is a reduction in lean body tissue or in body water. The only proven way to reduce body fat is to make lifestyle changes that include different eating behaviors and increased levels of physical activity.

Spot Reduction

Spot reduction is not possible. Individuals cannot lose fat from a specific location on the body. In one study, subjects did 5,000 sit-ups over a 27-day period; afterward, fat biopsies showed no preferential loss of fat in the abdominal area (Riposo, 1990). Exercises for specific parts of the body may strengthen the muscles there, but they have no effect on fat. Fat that is burned during exercise comes from all over the body in a genetically predetermined pattern.

Saunas and Steambaths

Saunas and steambaths produce weight loss by using heat to induce sweating. Since only water weight is lost, the pounds are regained quickly when fluid is restored by drinking.

Saunas and steambaths may be dangerous for the elderly and people suffering from diabetes, heart disease, or high blood pressure. Risks increase with the use of alcohol, drugs, and certain medications.

Body Wraps

In some reduction programs, bandages are soaked in a "magic" solution and wrapped tightly around the body. While this may compress the skin and move body fluids around, the change in body size is temporary. There is no actual weight loss.

Nonporous Sweatsuits

Plastic or rubberized garments produce temporary weight loss by inducing sweating. Again, however, this is water weight being lost; it will be regained quickly. When worn during exercise, such garments increase the risk of dehydration and heat-related injury.

Vibrating Belts

These and other passive mechanical devices, such as motor-driven toning machines and bicycles, do not induce weight loss or contribute to fitness. Vibrating belts may even be harmful when used on the abdomen, especially by women who are pregnant, menstruating, or using an IUD.

Diet Pills

Most diet pills sold over the counter contain phenylpropanolamine (PPA), which is a chemical relative to amphetamines or speed. Diet pills temporarily decrease appetite; typically, any weight loss is rapidly regained when the user stops taking them. Besides the danger of dependency, diet pills with PPA cause a sharp, potentially dangerous increase in blood pressure, and heart abnormalities also have been reported.

Fasting

Diet programs that severely restrict caloric intake should only be undertaken under direct medical supervision. **Fasting** results in the loss of large amounts of water, minerals, and lean body tissue, such as muscle. It also results in a minimal amount of fat loss. Prolonged fasting may cause dizziness and fainting, gout, anemia, kidney damage, hair loss, muscle cramping, reduced physical capabilities, emotional disturbances, and even death. Most people who reduce by fasting or through very-low calorie diets tend to regain much or all of the weight lost.

A change in dietary habits or physical activity aids in weight control and weight loss. A combination of diet and exercise is the ultimate weight-loss program.

Approaches to Weight Loss

Diet

Controlling diet by itself results in weight loss, even when daily caloric restriction is fairly modest. For example, if a dieter were to eat consistently over a long period of time 100 fewer calories a day (the equivalent of one bran muffin, one tablespoon of peanut butter, or one Bartlett pear), he or she would have a 700-calorie-per-week deficit. Since a deficit of 3,500 calories is needed to lose one pound of body fat, the dieter would lose a pound every five weeks, or ten pounds in a year.

Unfortunately, few people are patient enough to accept such a gradual weight loss. Instead, most are likely to restrict caloric intake substantially when beginning a diet. While they may have initial success, the weight usually is regained in the long run for several reasons.

First, it is difficult to stay on a low-calorie diet for a long period of time, and also it is unhealthy. Adequate essential nutrients may be lacking in diets that furnish fewer than 2,000 calories a day. Initial weight loss is a result of the depletion of carbohydrate stores in body fat and is quickly regained if normal eating resumes.

A second set of problems with dieting has to do with the "energy-out" side of the equation. The body "spends" at least two-thirds of its energy on basal metabolism, which includes all the processes that go on inside the body to support life, such as heartbeat, breathing, nerve and muscle impulses, and metabolic activity of cells. The remainder is spent on physical activity, or if unneeded, stored as fat.

The body has an internal mechanism to protect itself against starvation. When food intake is restricted, physiological changes cause a decrease in **basal metabolic rate (BMR).** In other words, the body automatically conserves energy, which causes a less effective diet. Over a period of time, weight loss by diet alone can cause a significant loss of lean body mass (LBM). Since LBM is more active metabolically than fat, the effect is to reduce BMR even further.

And finally, since dieters often feel tired and lethargic, they also tend to decrease physical activity, further lowering the output side of the equation.

Exercise

Exercise by itself also produces weight loss. A 150-pound person who walks at a normal pace for one-half hour, five times a week, burns 810 calories a week and achieves a weight loss of about 1 pound (a 3,500-calorie deficit) in about 30 days. If food consumption remains the same, this modest exercise program results in a loss of 12 pounds in a year.

The best exercise program for weight loss involves aerobic, endurance-type activities. With regular exercise, some of the factors that tilt the energy balance toward the deficit side are:

1. *Increase expenditure for physical activity*—Not only are more calories burned during physical activity, but energy expenditure has been shown to remain elevated for several hours afterward.
2. *Increase BMR*—Aerobic exercise increases the use of fatty acids for fuel in the muscles and speeds up the release of fat from storage. Exercise also increases bone mass and muscle density. The result is a change in body composition. Since LBM is more metabolically active than fat, exercise increases BMR, even at rest.
3. *Reduce appetite*—Moderate aerobic exercise has been shown to slightly depress the appetite.

Diet and Exercise Combined

By combining diet and exercise—reducing calorie intake by 100 calories a day and walking for 30 minutes, five times a week—our hypothetical 150-pound person could lose 22 pounds per year. People who incorporate regular aerobic exercise in a weight-loss program lose more weight than those who do not.

Combining diet and exercise also protects against the loss of lean tissue, eliminates the constant hunger and psychological stress of food deprivation, and allows for flexibility in a weight-loss regimen.

Set-Point Theory

The **set-point theory** states that the body has an internal regulating mechanism that strives to maintain a certain biologically determined body-fat level. In other words, when body-fat stores drop below a certain level, or set point, either because of dieting or starvation, the body automatically reacts to conserve energy by lowering BMR and increasing appetite. When fat stores are above the set point, the body will seek to lower them by decreasing appetite and increasing BMR, or by "wasting" energy. This theory purports to explain why so many people who lose weight by dieting tend to gain it back, and why other people can eat large amounts of food and remain slim.

Heredity, activity level, cigarette smoking, eating habits, and other factors combine to determine an individual's set point. While food deprivation tends to elevate the set point, exercise appears to lower it. Though many other factors are involved, the set-point theory implies that exercise, rather than calorie restriction, should be the first line of treatment for the overweight.

KEY WORDS

Nutrition
Nutrients
Minerals
Calories
Cholesterol

Sodium
Protein
Fiber
Body fat
Spot reduction

Fasting
Carbohydrate
Basal metabolic rate (BMR)
Set-point theory

SUMMARY

- The most important thing a student can do to enhance his or her state of health is maintain proper nutrition.
- Water is the most essential nutrient and also the most important in relation to physical performance.
- The U.S. Food and Drug Administration developed four classifications of foods: fruits and vegetables, grain products, milk and milk products, and meats and meat substitutes.
- The recommended servings from the basic four food groups furnish approximately 1200 to 1500 calories per day and adequate amounts of essential nutrients if a variety of foods are selected.
- When considering the issues of body weight and body fat, think of the body as being composed of two distinct parts: (1) lean body mass, and (2) fat body mass.
- It is not possible to lose fat from a specific location on the body.
- A combination of diet and exercise results in the ultimate weight-loss program.
- The set-point theory states that the body has an internal regulating mechanism that strives to maintain a certain biologically determined body-fat level.

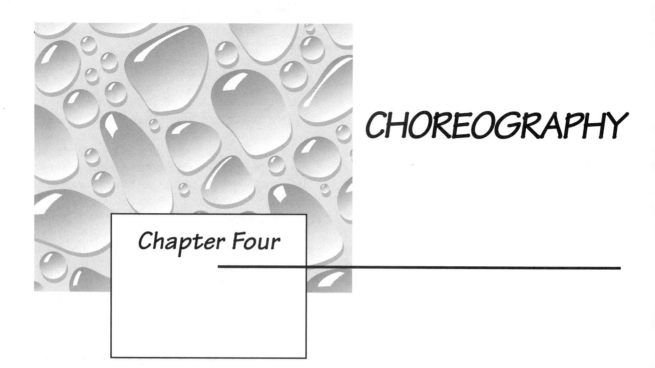

CHOREOGRAPHY

Chapter Four

MUSCLE BALANCE

Muscle imbalances reflect differences in the relative strengths and flexibilities of the various muscles surrounding a joint or body part. Muscle imbalances occur when some body segments are much more developed than others. Besides adversely affecting shock absorption, muscle imbalances can predispose a person to spasm, pain, injury, and faulty coordination.

The human body is designed to be balanced in all ways. Muscle groups work in **muscle pairs,** *agonists* and *antagonists*. In daily living, a person frequently uses one **muscle group** more than its paired muscle group, resulting in muscular imbalance. Imbalance between agonist and antagonist pairs results in elongated, weak muscles across one surface of a joint and shortened, strong muscles across the other. This, coupled with the aging process, may limit function and cause much of the pain aging people experience. Eventually, this stresses the **skeletal framework,** leading to more frequent pain, injury complexities, and sometimes extensive disability.

Typical muscles that are shortened and strong include:

1. anterior chest wall muscles (pectorals)
2. back extensor muscles (erector spinae)
3. muscles of the front of the thigh (iliopsoas)
4. calf muscles (gastrocnemius)
5. anterior upper-arm muscles (biceps)

Often elongated and weak are the abdominals, the upper-back muscles (trapezius and rhomboids), the shin muscles (tibialis anterior), the buttocks muscles (gluteals), and the posterior upper-arm muscles (triceps).

Anterior chest wall muscles that are tighter or shorter than normal cause the shoulders to become rounded, which can result in poor posture, neck pain, and limited chest expansion. The combination of tight erector spinae with iliopsoas and weak abdominals and gluteals is a major cause of back pain. Muscle-balanced workouts can decrease these problems.

The most important factor, then, in successful aquatic exercise programming is a basic understanding of why each movement is used. An aquatic program should not be haphazardly thrown together but carefully planned to consider muscle balance and safety. Giving each move a purpose greatly increases the quality of an aquatic exercise program. Good programs also include movements that are simply fun. Nonetheless, aquatic instructors should examine fun moves to make sure they do not compromise muscle balance and safety.

When creating a program, **muscle balance** should always be considered. This means that each of the major muscle groups should be worked with two or three moves in every workout. Instructors should remember to work **opposing muscles** of a pair at least equally. If the program includes 16 bicep curls, it should also include 16 tricep extensions. If students are doing lots of kicks, kneelifts, and jogging with knees up, they will be strengthening and tightening the hip flexors. They should do an equal number of moves to work the gluteals.

The exception to equal work is when one partner of a muscle group is weaker than the other. Then it is accepted practice to use the weak muscle more extensively than the strong one. In other words, it is okay to use more moves that include the traditionally weaker muscles (triceps, abdominals, gluteals, and tibialis anterior) and fewer moves that use the traditionally stronger muscles (biceps, spinae erector, iliopsoas, and gastrocnemius). Instructors should make sure, however, the stronger of each pair is not ignored completely.

Since the stronger muscle in each pair is simpler to work, there is always the tendency to encourage existing muscle imbalance, doing only easy (kneelifts, jogs, jog arms) moves and trying to compensate in the toning section. Unfortunately, 10 to 15 minutes of toning cannot undo the muscle imbalance caused by everyday life. As a fitness professional, the instructor needs to assist students in overall health and wellness. In order to do that, the entire program should be well thought out in terms of why moves are used and if they assist in overall muscle balance.

Safety is another reason for knowing why a move is used. If an instructor is using movement to strengthen gluteals but finds that it may compromise the low back or is possibly a **contraindicated** move, he or she should modify it or replace it with a safer movement. Thinking about each move keeps the program top notch.

CONTRAINDICATED EXERCISES

Aquatic exercise programs tend to have a large variety of populations and body types. For that reason, exercises that are safe for one person may not be for another.

Some exercise is **generally contraindicated,** which means that it is harmful to the exerciser's physical well-being. This means that the exercise is contraindicated for everyone. **Relatively contraindicated** means that the exercise is contraindicated for some individuals.

To create the safest possible program, an aquatic exerciser should be aware of two specific concepts when doing programming or choreography:

1. *The purpose of each exercise*—With this knowledge, moves that may aggravate some students' conditions can be replaced with other moves that have the same exercise purpose. For instance, a prone flutter kick primarily works the hip flexors (iliopsoas) and elevates heartrate. Since prone flutter kicks have a high risk potential, an instructor could replace them with standing forward kicks, which have a lower risk potential but still work the hip flexors (iliopsoas) and elevate heartrate. If forward kicks aggravate a student's low back, the forward kicks could be changed to kneelifts, which also work the hip flexors and elevate heartrate.

2. *High-risk areas in the average body*—The student must be aware of specific areas to protect. Always compare the ratio of benefits of an exercise to its risk. If the benefit outweighs the risk, the student should use the move. There is risk associated with every type of move. Only those that seem to be high risk or cause discomfort should be eliminated.

High-Risk Areas

High-risk areas include knees, shoulders, neck, low back, ankles, and feet.

Knees. Knees can be protected by remembering that their function is simple flexion and extension. Safe moves for the knee joint will not hyperextend it, twist it, move it too quickly, or overflex it.

Movements should be slow and controlled when the knee joint is involved. Ballistic or percussive movements in the knee can cause injury. Extremely fast flexion and extension can cause damage to the joint capsule, tendons, and ligaments. Students sometimes use excessively fast movements during the toning portion at the end of class to feel the muscles working. Using force rather than speed during toning ensures a better and safer workout.

Shoulders. Shoulder impingement has become a concern of low-impact aerobic students. It also should be a concern of aquatic exercise instructors and students. Seventy percent of the U.S. population has degenerative shoulder problems.

Shoulder impingement can occur in aquatic exercise when students spend a sustained period of time hanging from their arms on kickboards or at the edge of the pool, using the arms overhead excessively or vigorously, and moving arms in and out of the water repeatedly.

Neck. The **cervical vertebrae** and discs can be injured during aquatic exercise. The cervical area of the spine has several functions, including flexion and extension (bending and straightening), lateral flexion (sideways tilting), and rotation (turning). A safe rule for aquatic exercise instructors is to allow the cervical area of the spine to move in only one of those directions at a time. This is a conservative way of viewing each of the moves the students do.

Hyperextension of the cervical area of the spine should be eliminated from aquatic exercises. Students look up but not all the way up. Full-neck circles should be eliminated and replaced with a look down, a look somewhat up, a look to the right, then left, and a neck stretch (with the right ear to the right shoulder and then, the left ear to the left shoulder). Percussive or ballistic moves in the cervical area of the spine also can damage the vertebrae and discs.

Low Back. Eighty to ninety percent of the population in North America experiences back pain at some time in their lives. Low-back pain is the most common problem. For that reason, exercises involving the low-back muscles should be well thought out.

The lumbar and thoracic areas of the spine have several functions. They can do spinal flexion and extension (bending forward and returning), lateral flexion (sidebends), and rotation (twisting). A good rule is to allow the back to do only one of these functions at a time. Hyperextension of the lumbar area of the spine should be eliminated from all standing or moving exercises.

Many of the exercises that compromise the low back are those thought to work the abdominals, so students work them more vigorously and enthusiastically than they do other exercises. Very few abdominal exercises actually compromise the low back. The exercises that students and instructors think work the abdominals actually are working the iliopsoas or hip flexors. Instructors should be aware that if the spine (vertebrae) is flexing, the abdominals are working. The **Aquatic Exercise Association** has an aquatic abdominal video workshop; see page 121 for the Association's address. If the hip joint is moving, the muscles working are the iliopsoas. Double-leg lifts and flutter kicks both work the iliopsoas. A safer way to work the iliopsoas is with standing forward kicks.

All exercises involving the lumbar area of the spine should be slow and controlled. Ballistic or percussive moves can easily cause injury in the low-back area. **Sustained spinal flexion** is not encouraged in any type of exercise for the general population.

Lower Leg, Foot, and Ankle. The lower leg, foot, and ankle are susceptible to many overuse injuries. Even though these injuries are impressively lessened by working out in the water, they still can occur. Many injuries are associated with students' specific anatomy. A person with excessive **pronation** (rolling in) of the foot is more likely to have an injury on the inside or medial side of the leg or ankle. **Supinators** (students who roll out), however, are more likely to have an injury on the outside or lateral portion of the lower leg or ankle.

Side-to-side movements need to be done with control and stability. Many other ankle/foot injuries are caused by impact. The in-structor can guard against this in three ways: (1) moving students to deeper water; (2) adding a flotation belt or vest; and (3) creating a program with less bouncing and more walking or traveling moves.

Impact injuries also can be lessened by learning how to land. Students who stay on the forefoot can develop severe lower-leg and foot injuries. Consciously thinking about landing first on the forefoot and rolling the heel down to the bottom of the pool and bending the knee can decrease considerably the likelihood of injury. Adding shoes that are designed for aquatic exercise or aerobics can protect the foot and ankle and protect the bottoms of the feet from having an excessive amount of skin worn away, and from slipping.

Repetitions

Excessive reps of one move that causes bouncing on the other leg can lead to an overuse injury and cause the support leg to become destabi-lized. It is prudent to bounce only eight times on one foot before changing to the other. Toning exercises where no bouncing on the other foot occurs can be repeated up to 30 or 40 times.

Traveling Moves

Lateral, forward, or backward movement increases the intensity of a workout. Traveling also can increase workout risk. To minimize risk, remember proper alignment before beginning a traveling move.

Tempo

The speed, or **tempo**, of the exercise or music should allow enough time to move each exercise through a full range of motion in a controlled manner. Percussive, ballistic, or jerky types of movements can cause injuries throughout the body.

Preventive Measures

Good shoes, specifically designed for the type of aquatic exercise being performed, are essential for injury prevention and assist in keeping injuries from recurring. Shoes should fit the shape of the student's foot, have adequate cushioning in the heel and forefoot to absorb shock, and be well padded in the arch. The shoes also should have good stability for forward, backward, and lateral movement, and the heel box should be firm for heel stability. Shoes also should have good flexibility to move with the foot. The flexion should be near the toes, not at the arch. The sole of the shoe should have adequate gripping power to hold on slippery pool bottoms. Comfort, fit, cushioning, stability, flexibility, and gripping are the characteristics of a good aquatic shoe.

A gradual progression, from warm-up and stretching to higher-intensity activity and gradual recovery and stretching at the end of class, also reduces the likelihood of injury recurrence. Individual pacing and progressive overload must continually be kept in mind. While variety of movement is important, tricky steps and awkward transitions should be avoided. Continuous reps of the same movement have little value during the aerobic portion of the class and can lead to overuse injuries. Staying in any one position, out of proper alignment, for too long also has the potential for harm. Students should not whip, hurl, or flail body parts but rather move slowly with control and always be aware of how they feel. Any movement that causes pain should be eliminated.

Maintaining good alignment allows muscles to work without strain and assists in preventing injury recurrence. Good alignment allows the safe transfer of body weight and enables the joints and spine to absorb shock efficiently. Participants should think about "standing tall" when exercising. **Footstrikes** should not be done with the toes only but should begin on the toes and allow the heels to contact the pool bottom while rolling through the foot. The knees and hips should bend each time jumping, bouncing, or landing occurs.

A CATALOG OF MOVEMENTS

Moves are listed in alphabetical order for convenience. Major muscle groups involved are listed in the description of each movement. Many moves begin in one of the basic positions listed here.

Starting Positions

- *Feet Together*—stand, with the feet lined up, neither foot forward of the other, and no more than six inches apart
- *Prone*—lie on the water surface in a face-down position
- *Stride Position*—stand, with the feet shoulder-width apart, toes and knees pointed forward
- *Supine*—Lie on the water surface in a face-up position

Arm Movements

Suggested arm movements are often listed for step movements, and step movements are often listed with arm movements. Arm movements may use the following terms:

- *Corresponding or Opposite*—*Corresponding* refers to movements in which the arm and leg on the same side of the body move together, in the same direction. *Opposite* refers to movements in which the arm on one side of the body moves in the same direction as the leg on the other side of the body.

- *Doubles and Singles*—*Doubles* indicates that both arms move together with the same movement, in the same direction. *Singles* indicates that only one arm is doing the movement.

All the moves listed in this section of the book can be used with all types of choreography (see end of chapter) and in any type of program (i.e., deep water, interval training, aerobics, sports conditioning).

Individual Moves

Abdominal Stretch

While standing, lift the ribs and push the rib cage forward. This will cause a slight hyperextension of the lumbar area of the spine. Use with caution.

— Abdominal Stretch

Adductor Stretch

Take a big step to the left, with the toes of both feet pointed forward. The feet will be more than shoulder-width apart. Bend the left knee, but keep the right knee straight. This will stretch the adductors in the right leg. If the water is too deep for this stretch to be effective, lift the right knee up and to the right to stretch the right adductor. Reverse to stretch the left leg adductor.

— Adductor Stretch (version 1)

— Adductor Stretch (version 2)

— Abductor Stretch

Abductor Stretch

While standing on one foot, pull the heel of the right foot toward the front of the hip of the left leg. Press the right knee in toward the left shoulder for the Abductor Stretch right. Reverse for Abductor Stretch left.

Anterior Deltoid Stretch

See Bicep, Anterior Deltoid, and Pectoral Stretch.

Anterior Tibialis Stretch

See Iliopsoas Stretch.

Armswing Forward

Begin with the arms down at the sides, palms back (pronated). Lift both arms forward through the water with force until the arms are extended in front of the body, just beneath the water surface. This portion of the move works the deltoids and pectorals. Keeping palms down, press both arms back to the beginning position. This portion of the move works the deltoids and latissimus dorsi. Proper body alignment should be maintained during the Armswings. This move can be varied by alternately swinging one arm forward and the other backward.

Armswing Forward Flexed

Begin with arms the down at the sides, elbows bent (flexed) at a 90- to 120-degree angle, and palms back (pronated). Lift both arms forward through the water, maintaining the original elbow flexion, until the arms are in front of the body, just beneath the water surface. This portion of the move works the deltoids, biceps, and pectorals. Keeping the palms down, press both arms back to the beginning position. This portion of the move works the deltoids, biceps, and latissimus dorsi. This move can be varied by alternately swinging one arm forward and the other backward.

Armswing Side

Begin with the arms down at the sides, palms back (pronated). Move both arms to the right and then up toward the water surface to the right. This is Armswing right. Return the arms to the beginning position. Move both arms to the left and then up toward the water surface to the left. This is Armswing left. Return the arms to the beginning position. This move can be varied in several ways. Armswing right with the right arm only and Armswing left with the left arm only is a Single (one arm only) Corresponding (the same side) Armswing right or left. The elbow can be slightly flexed to create variety. Palms can be pronated so hands slice through the water, or they can push through the water with the backs of the hands leading

— Armswing Forward

— Armswing Forward Flexed

— Armswing Side

or with the palms cupped and leading for added resistance. Armswing Side works the deltoids, pectorals, and trapezius.

Back Kick

Begin with the feet in stride position, arms at the sides. Without flexing (bending) the knee, kick the right leg back (hip hyperextension). Return to the beginning position, and repeat the movement with the left leg. To protect the lower back, the right arm should swing forward, punch forward, or elbow press when the right leg kicks back. Both arms can swing, punch, or press forward when either leg kicks back. It is not advisable to move the arms back when the leg is moving back, since it may compromise the lower back. Back Kicks can be done slowly, with a bounce

between each one, or quickly, kicking one out while the other returns. Another variation is alternating the kicks right and left or doing them in groups of two, four, or eight right before changing to the left leg. Back Kicks work the gluteals and iliopsoas.

Back-Kick Swing

Begin with the feet in stride position. Kick the right leg forward (hip flexion) for the first count, and swing it straight back to slight hip hyperextension for the second count. The Back-Kick Swing gives a larger range of motion while working the gluteals than the Back Kick. Abdominal muscles should be contracted while the leg is swinging back for back safety, and the work should be felt in the gluteals. The Back-Kick

Swing works the iliopsoas and gluteals. It can be done alternating right and left legs or in groups of two, four, or eight with one leg before switching to the other. The left arm should swing forward as the right leg kicks forward, and the right arm should swing forward as the right leg swings back to avoid compromising the lower back.

Back Lunge

Begin with the feet in stride position, arms extended laterally (out to the sides), with palms facing forward. Step the right foot back, and shift the body weight to the right foot, keeping the left foot down in beginning position. During the step back, move the arms forward just beneath the water surface until palms almost

▬ Back Kick

▬ Back-Kick Swing (position 1)

▬ Back-Kick Swing (position 2)

– Back Lunge

meet. Return the right foot to the beginning position, while pressing the arms back to the beginning position. Repeat with the left foot. This move works the gluteals, iliopsoas, pectorals, and trapezius.

Back Stretch

Begin facing the pool edge, with the hands and arms extended over it. Bring the knees to the chest, and hug them. See also Erector Spinae Stretch.

Back Touch

See Touch Back.

Backstroke

Begin with both elbows in at the waist and the forearms out to side for the **Short Back-stroke**. With the palm supinated (facing forward) and the elbow flexed and staying in at waist, reach back with the hand, cup the water, and pull it forward (almost a complete circumduction of the elbow). This can be done alternating the right and left arms or using

– Short Backstroke

– Long Backstroke

both together. The **Short Backstroke** works biceps and triceps. The **Long Backstroke** is the same move with arms extended. Both arms begin extended laterally, with palms down, just beneath the water surface. Reach back, turn the palm to face front, cup the water, and pull it down and forward. This move works the deltoids, trapezius, and pectorals. It can be done alternating the right and left arms or doing both at one time. Both back-strokes are excellent means of moving back through the water.

Backstroke Side

With the right arm extended just below the water surface, back to the right (behind the body), with a slight flex in the elbow and the palm facing right,

– Backstroke Side

pull the right arm forward and left (still just below the water surface) until it is extended directly in front of the body. Return to the beginning position, and repeat with the left arm extended back to the left and moving forward. This move works pectorals, serratus anterior, deltoids, rhomboids, and trapezius. Performing the same move using the forearm only (the action will be in the elbow, not the shoulder) will work biceps and triceps. It can be performed using both arms at once in either manner. It works well with any ordinarily stationary move, either done in place or moving backwards.

Baseball Swing

Using both arms, swing back to the right and then forward, as though hitting a baseball. Repeat on the left side.

Basketball Jump

Bounce three times in a low, crouched position, mimicking bouncing a basketball. Push up and out of the water as far as possible, mimicking shooting a basketball.

Bicep, Anterior Deltoid, and Pectoral Stretch

With the fingers interlaced, low behind the back, turn the elbows in toward each other, and lift the arms up behind the back until a stretch is felt in the pectorals, anterior deltoids, and biceps. Keep the chest out, the chin in, and the back straight.

— Bicep, Anterior Deltoid, and Pectoral Stretch

Bicep Curl

Begin with the elbows in at the waist and the hands down, palms forward (supinated). Bend the elbows (elbow flexion) to a 45- to 90-degree angle

— Bicep Curl

for the first count. Return to the beginning position for the second count. This is one Bicep Curl. Bicep Curls can be done singly (8 to 16 with one arm before switching to the other arm); this is often done during toning. They can also be done alternating right and left arms. Bicep Curls work the biceps.

Boogie

Begin with the feet in stride position. Step the right foot behind and to the left of the left foot, while the left foot remains stationary. The torso faces forward or may twist slightly to the left while the exerciser looks to the left. Reach the left arm down to the left diagonal; pull the right arm out of the water, and reach up to the right diagonal. This is the first count. Return to the beginning position for the second count. Step the left foot behind and to the right

— Boogie

of the right foot. Look to the right and keep the torso either facing forward or slightly twisted to the right. Reach the right arm down to the right diagonal; pull the left arm out of the water, and reach up to the left diagonal. This is the third count. Return to beginning position for the fourth count. These four counts represent one set of Boogie. The Boogie works obliques, adductors, and gluteals. It can be done four or eight times with the right foot before changing to the left. The arm movements can be varied; keep them beneath the water surface by using Press Down Front arms.

Bow and Arrow

Begin with both arms extended laterally (out to the side) to the left side at shoulder level. Feet, knees, hips, and shoulders are pivoted to the left to allow the palms to begin together. With feet, knees, and hips stationary, pull the right elbow back until the right fist is near the right shoulder. (To eliminate the oblique work for people with back problems, allow the feet, knees, and hips to pivot with the shoulders.) Continue with several repetitions, using the right arm before switching to the left. Pectorals, deltoids, trapezius, and rhomboids are all involved with this move.

Buffalo Shuffle

The Buffalo Shuffle moves laterally, doing four or eight shuffles to the right followed by four or eight to the left. Begin in stride position. Step the right foot to the right, with the knees, toes, and torso facing forward; kick the left foot out slightly to the left side. Move the right arm out of the water, and point to the right diagonal; keep the left arm on the left hip. This is the first count. Step the left foot behind the right foot, while bringing the right knee up. Bring the right elbow down to the water surface. This is the second count. Repeat counts 1

— Buffalo Shuffle (position 1)

— Bow and Arrow (position 1)

— Bow and Arrow (position 2)

— Buffalo Shuffle (position 2)

and 2 three or seven more times moving to the right.

For the Buffalo Shuffle left, step laterally to the left with the left foot while the knees, toes, and torso face forward; kick the right leg out slightly to the right. Move the left arm out of the water, and point to the left diagonal; keep the right hand on the right hip. This is the first count. Step the right foot behind the left foot, while bringing the left knee up. Bring the left elbow down to the water surface. This is the second count. Repeat counts 1 and 2 three or seven more times to complete a set of the Buffalo Shuffle left. The Buffalo Shuffle works adductors and abductors.

Calf Stretch

See Gastrocnemius Stretch.

Cross Kick

Begin with the feet in stride position, with the right hip slightly rotated externally (right toes will be pointed to the right diagonal). Cross and lift the right heel in front and to the left of the left ankle. Return to the beginning position. With the left hip slightly rotated externally (left toes will be pointed to the left diagonal), cross the left heel in front and to the right of the right ankle. Return to the beginning position. The Cross Kick works adductors and abductors. The move must be made with the heel leading through the water. If the hip rotates internally and the toes point to the opposite diagonal

⚊ Cross Kick

and lead the move, the iliopsoas will be involved. The torso should be kept facing forward. Lateral push to the right when the right leg is crossing to the left and vice versa.

Cross Rock

The Cross Rock is much like the Rocking Horse done with the legs in a crossed position. Begin with the weight on the left foot and the right leg lifted (hip flexion) slightly across the left leg. Step the right foot forward and across the left foot, leaning forward toward the left (over the right foot) but keeping the body straight. Avoid any spinal flexion that might cause the body to bend at the waist. Bring the left foot up, off the pool bottom, and kick back slightly to the right, shifting the weight to the right foot. This is the first count. Step the

⚊ Cross Rock (position 1)

⚊ Cross Rock (position 2)

left foot back to the beginning position, and lean slightly back to the right, keeping the body straight. Avoid any spinal hyperextension that might cause the body to bend backward at the waist. Bring the right foot up, off the pool bottom, and kick forward to the left; shift the weight to the left leg. This is the second count. Repeat counts 1 and 2 three more times and then switch to Cross Rock left, with the left foot rocking forward and across the right foot and the right foot rocking back and to the left. The Cross Rock works iliopsoas, gluteals, obliques, and abdominals. Safe Arms, pushing back as the body leans or rocks forward and pushing forward as the body rocks back, work well with this move (see Safe Arms). This move can be varied to Cross Rock Doubles, Cross Rock in Three, or Cross Rock Seven and Up (as described in Rocking Horse sections) when done with a crossing rock.

Crossing Jog

The Crossing Jog moves laterally to the left in sets of four or eight and then returns to the right. Begin with the feet in stride position, hands on hips. Cross the right foot over and toward the left of the left foot; shift the weight to the right foot while lifting the left foot slightly off the pool bottom. This is the first count. Step the left foot to the left of the right foot; shift the weight to the left foot. This is the second count. Repeat counts 1 and 2 three or seven more times while moving sideways through the water to the left. Reverse by crossing the left foot over the right and shifting the weight to the left foot for the first count. Step the right foot laterally to the right of the left foot; shift the weight to the

– Crossing Jog

right foot for the second count. Repeat counts 1 and 2 three or seven more times while moving right. The arms can stay on the hips or push laterally (to the right when moving left, to the left when moving right). Keep the torso facing forward to achieve the excellent oblique, adductor, and abductor work this move provides.

The Crossing Jog can also be done with the leading foot crossing behind instead of in front, as described above. While moving left, the right foot would step behind the left foot for the first count of each two-count segment. While moving right, the left foot would behind the right foot during the first count of each two-count segment. This is called Crossing Jog behind and also works the adductors and abductors. The Crossing Jog in front and behind can be

combined to create a grapevine move. A two-count segment of Crossing Jog in front moving left would be followed by a two-count segment of Crossing Jog behind moving left; repeat twice before reversing to move to the right. This can be called a Crossing Jog Combo or a Grapevine. The cues would be "cross, step, back, step, cross, step, back, step."

Crossing Legswing

Begin standing, with the back to the pool edge. Lift the right leg (hip flexion) until it is at a 90-degree angle, with the knee slightly flexed (bent). Cross (horizontally adduct) the right leg toward the pool edge on the left side of the body. This is the first count. Return the leg to the beginning (forward) position for the second count. Swing the leg out (horizontally abduct) toward the pool edge on the right side of the body. This is the third count. Return it to beginning position for the fourth count. This is one Crossing Legswing. Repeat seven more times with the right leg before switching to the left leg for eight more. The Crossing Legswing works the adductors and abductors. **This move can severely compromise the stability of the weight-bearing knee**. If this move is used, the weight-bearing knee should be slightly flexed and never feel any twisting movement. The range of motion for the Crossing Legswing should be very small. The Kneeswing Cross-

– Crossing Legswing (position 1)

– Curl Down

– Deltoid Lift

– Crossing Legswing (position 2)

ing may be a better choice for adductor and abductor work.

Curl Down

Begin with the arms extended (shoulder flexion) straight in front of the body, just below the water surface. Bend forward (forward spinal flexion) at the waist, bringing the sternum and navel closer together. Return to an upright position. As the

spine bends forward, keep the shoulders and elbows tight; the arms will be forced down, deeper into the water. The arms themselves should not do the moving (avoid any shoulder extension) but only move because of the spinal flexion. The arms will create a drag and force the abdominal muscles to work during the flexion. Students should be cautioned not to bend at the hips, as this will work the already strong iliopsoas muscles. The bend or flexion should occur only at the waist. Holding a buoyant device (milk jug, kickboard, ball, etc.) in the hands will increase the difficulty of the abdominal work.

Deltoid Lift

Begin with both arms down at the sides, palms in at the thighs (supinated). Lift the arms with force to the sides and up (abduct). This portion of the move focuses on the deltoids. To reverse the move, press both arms

down through the water. This portion of the move works the latissimus dorsi.

Deltoid Stretch (Medial)

Begin with a Neck Stretch (see Neck Stretch). When the head is tilted to the left side, reach behind the back with the left arm, and pull gently on the

– Deltoid Stretch (Medial)

right wrist. Reverse for the Deltoid Stretch left.

Deltoid Stretch (Posterior)

With the right arm at shoulder level, pull the right elbow in toward the chest with the left hand, and bend the right elbow to feel the stretch in the posterior deltoids. Reverse for the Posterior Deltoid Stretch left.

▬ Deltoid Stretch (Posterior)

Diagonal Kick

See Kick Corner.

Elbow Press

Begin with both arms out to the sides (extended laterally). The elbows are flexed to 90 degrees, with the forearms straight up from the elbows. Lower the arms into the water. Begin the move in this position.

Press the elbows and hands toward each other (shoulder adduction) until they almost

▬ Elbow Press

touch. Pull them apart to return to the beginning of the move. The press works the pectorals and serratus anterior, while the pull works the rhomboids and trapezius. Jogging, Mule Kicks, and Heel Tilts all work well with these arm movements (see Mule Kick and Heel Tilt). Be sure the arms are kept below the water surface, if possible.

Elbow Press Single

Begin with both arms out to the sides (extended laterally). The elbows are flexed to 90 degrees, with the forearms straight up from the elbows. Lower the arms into the water. Begin the move in this position. Press the right elbow across the body (shoulder adduction) to the left elbow, which has not moved. Stop and pull the elbow back to the beginning position (shoulder abduction). Repeat with the right arm, if desired, and then

▬ Elbow Press Single

with the left arm. Swing Twists work well with these arms (see Swing Twist).

Elbow Press with Forearm Down

Begin with both arms out to the sides (extended laterally). The elbows are flexed to a 90- to

▬ Elbow Press with Forearm Down

140-degree angle with the forearms straight down from the elbows. This will cause forward (anterior) shoulder rotation in most people. Widen the angle until no shoulder stress is experienced. Begin the move in this position. Press the elbows and hands back toward each other, reaching behind the body. This works the rhomboids and trapezius. Bring the arms forward to return to the beginning position.

Erector Spinae Stretch

With the toes and knees pointed forward and the feet shoulder-width apart, put the hands on the front of the thighs. Pull the abdominals in, and arch the back to feel the stretch. If the water is too deep, the stretch can be done with the hands interlaced and pushing forward.

— Erector Spinae Stretch

Flag Arms

Begin with the hands on the hips and the elbows out to the

— Flag Arms

sides. While keeping the elbow in position, lift the forearm forward and up until it points straight up. The fingertips should be just beneath the water surface. This rotates the right shoulder externally. The left forearm moves down and back while the left elbow retains position. The left forearm should point straight down. This internally rotates the left shoulder. This is the first position of Flag Arms. Reverse by pressing the right forearm forward and down (internally rotating the shoulder) and lifting the left forearm forward and straight up (externally rotating the left shoulder). This is the second position of Flag Arms. Repeat positions 1 and 2 to work the shoulder rotator cuff, deltoids, and trapezius.

Flick Kick

Begin with the weight on the left leg and the right hip externally rotated (turned out). Flex

the right knee and extend (bend and straighten) four times. This is Flick Kick–4. Repeat with the left leg. The Flick Kick works the quadriceps and hamstrings. To increase the work on the quadriceps, move forward to the right or right diagonal during the Flick Kick right. To increase the work on the hamstrings, move back.

— Flick Kick (position 1)

— Flick Kick (position 2)

Fling

Begin with the weight on the left leg and the right hip externally rotated (turned out). Flex (bend) the right knee to about a 90-degree angle. Begin the move in this position. Lift the right heel forward as high as possible, while maintaining the knee flexion, hip flexion, and proper body alignment. The left (opposite) arm can come out of the water and reach overhead or stay underwater and press from abduction (arm straight out to the side just beneath the water surface) toward the right heel. Step the right foot down, and repeat with the left foot and right arm. The Fling can be done slowly, with both feet bouncing together between each move, or it can be done quickly, with the left heel lifting while the right one is returning, and vice versa. The Fling can also be done in groups of two, four, or eight right before switching to the left leg.

Fling Kick

Begin with the weight on the left foot and the right hip externally rotated (turned out). Flex (bend) the right knee to about a 120-degree angle. Begin the move in this position. Lift the right foot forward as high as possible, while maintaining the knee flexion, hip rotation, and proper body alignment. Step the right foot down, and repeat with the left leg. This move is much like a Kick with the toes pointed out (see Kick). To ensure adductor work, the heel and instep should lead. The Fling Kick can be done slowly, with both feet bouncing together between each kick, or quickly, with the left foot moving forward while the right foot is returning. It can be done in groups of two, four, or eight with the right leg before switching to the left leg. The Fling Kick works adductors and abductors. (See the Fling for optional arm movements.)

Flutter Kick

This move is usually done in a floating position with kickboards, jugs, or other buoyant devices under the arms. It is also frequently done in a prone position (lying on the stomach) with the hands on the pool edge. With knees locked in at about a 5-degree flexion (bend), flex and extend (bend and straighten) the hip. The right leg kicks forward as the left leg kicks back, and the left leg kicks forward as the right leg kicks back. This move works iliopsoas and gluteals. **This move can compromise the lower back (lumbar area of the spine) if done in a prone position with the face out of the water.**

Forward Lunge

Begin in stride position, with the arms extended forward (shoulder flexion) and the palms facing out (away from each

— Fling

— Fling Kick

— Forward Lunge

other). Step the right foot forward, and shift the body weight to the right foot while bending the right knee as the arms push straight back (as in Safe Arms). This is the first count. Step the right foot back to stride position, as the arms return to the beginning position. This is the second count. Repeat counts 1 and 2 with the left foot. This move works quadriceps, hamstrings, pectorals, rhomboids, and trapezius.

Forward Touch

See Touch Forward.

Forward Train

Begin with the feet in stride position, with arms forward, just beneath the water surface, and the palms back. Step the right foot forward and shift weight forward, while bending the right knee and pushing the arms back until they're extended laterally (out to the sides). Lift the left foot off the pool bottom, behind the left leg. This is the first count. Step the left foot back into the beginning position, while lifting the right knee and returning the arms to the beginning position. This is the second count. Step the right foot back and shift the body weight back onto the right foot, while lifting the left knee and pushing the arms forward and together. This is the third count. Step the left foot forward to the beginning position, while lifting the right knee and returning the arms to the beginning position. This is the fourth

count. This is one Forward Train with the right foot leading; repeat three more times. Then do Forward Train four times with the left foot leading. Forward Train works pectorals, rhomboids, trapezius, iliopsoas, and gluteals.

— Forward Train (position 1)

— Forward Train (position 3)

Frog Jump

Begin with the feet in stride position, the hips externally rotated (toes and knees pointed out). Pull both knees up toward the shoulders. This is one Frog Jump. Push both arms down in front or press them down be-

— Forward Train (position 2)

— Forward Train (position 4)

– Frog jump

hind during the Frog Jump. This move works the iliopsoas and gluteals. Maintain proper body alignment and a posterior pelvic tilt during the Frog Jumps.

Gastrocnemius Stretch

Take a big step forward, with the left foot in front of the body and the right foot behind. Be sure the toes of the right foot point forward or even slightly inward. The heels must be down on both feet. Lean forward slowly and hold, as the calf muscle of the back leg stretches.

– Gastrocnemius Stretch

If the buoyancy of the water makes it difficult to feel this stretch, think about pulling the toes of the back foot up. Reverse for Gastrocnemius Stretch left.

Gluteal Stretch

Pull the right knee toward the chest and hold it, with the hands under the knee (behind the thigh). Stand up straight on the left foot, which should be pointed straight ahead, with the knee slightly bent. Bring the knee up, as close to the chest as possible, and hold. Reverse for left Gluteal Stretch.

– Gluteal Stretch

Golfing

Use both arms to mimic a golfswing. Repeat on both the left and right sides of the body.

Hamstring Stretch

Stand, facing the pool edge. Put the bottom of the right foot against the pool side, or put the right heel into the pool gutter. Stand up straight. The left foot on the pool bottom should be pointed straight ahead, with the knee slightly bent. While looking straight ahead, bend forward at the waist, and then straighten the right leg until a stretch is felt in the back of the right thigh. Reverse for the left leg. An alternative Hamstring Stretch is to begin in the Gluteal Stretch position, with the knee tucked up, close to the chest. While keeping the knee close to the chest, straighten (extend) the leg until an easy stretch is felt in the hamstrings.

– Hamstring Stretch

Heel Diamond

Buoyancy is needed. In a supine position, place the insteps of the feet together. Keeping them together, flex the knees and hips a in lateral motion (pulling the heels toward the body), and return to a normal, semistraight position. This move works adductors and abductors.

Heel Hit Across

Bounce once on the left foot, while reaching the left hand back to touch the right heel as it pulls up in front of the body and to the right of the right hip (knee flexion with internal hip rotation). Bounce once on the right foot, while reaching the right hand back to touch the left heel as it pulls up in front of the body and to the left of the left hip. Heel Hit Across works the quadriceps and hamstrings. **This move can compromise the knee joint.** It is important to keep the torso tall and the spine straight during Heel Hits.

– Heel Hit Across

– Heel Hit Behind

Heel Hit Behind

Bounce once on the left foot, while reaching the left hand back to touch the right heel as it pulls up behind the left leg. Bounce once on the right foot, while reaching the right hand back to touch the left heel as it pulls up behind the right leg. Heel Hits Behind work the hamstrings and quadriceps. It is important to maintain proper body alignment with a posterior pelvic tilt to avoid compromising the lower back. It is important to keep the torso tall and the spine straight during Heel Hits.

Heel Hit Front

Bounce once on the left foot, while reaching the left hand down to touch the right heel as it pulls up in front of the left thigh. Bounce once on the right foot, while reaching the right

– Heel Hit Front

hand down to touch the left heel as it pulls up in front of the right thigh. Heel Hit Front works the adductors and abductors. It is important to keep the torso tall and the spine straight during Heel Hits.

Heel Jack

Begin with the feet in stride position. Bounce once on the left foot, while tilting slightly back to the left and touching the right heel forward to the right diagonal on the pool bottom. This is the first count. Bounce once with both feet together for the second count. Bounce once on the right foot, while tilting slightly back to the right and touching the left heel forward to the left diagonal on the pool bottom. This is the third count. Bounce once with both feet together for the fourth count. This is one set of

- Heel Jack

slow Heel Jacks. The arms can press down behind as the heel touches forward and out. Heel Jacks work the abdominals, obliques, and tibialis anterior. Heel Jacks can be done quickly by leaving out the second and fourth counts. During the fast Heel Jacks, punch the left arm through the water, down toward the right foot while the right heel touches. Punch the right arm through the water, down toward the left foot while the left heel touches.

Heel Jack in Three

Begin with the feet in stride position. Bounce once on the left foot, while tilting slightly back to the left and touching the right heel forward to the right diagonal to the pool bottom. This is the first count. Bounce once with both feet together for the second count.

Bounce once on the right foot, while tilting slightly back to the right and touching the left heel forward to the left diagonal to the pool bottom. This is the third count. Bounce with both feet together once for the fourth count. Bounce once on the left foot, while tilting slightly back to the left and touching the right heel forward to the right diagonal. This is the fifth count. Bounce both feet together once for the sixth count. Bounce once on the left foot, while tilting slightly back to the left and touching the right heel forward to the right diagonal. This is the seventh count. Bounce both feet together once for the eighth count. Cue as "right, bounce, left, bounce, right, bounce, right, bounce." Repeat the Heel Jack in Three to the left (counts 9 through 16), cueing as "left, bounce, right, bounce, left, bounce, left, bounce." The Heel Jack in Three can be done quickly by leaving out all of the even-numbered counts (all of the bounces done with the feet together).

Heel Tilt

Begin with the feet together. Touch the right heel forward, while tilting the body back slightly and bending the left knee. (The weight is on the left foot.) This is the first count. Step the right foot next to the left to return to the beginning position for the second count. Touch the left heel forward, while tilting the body back slightly and bending the right

- Heel Tilt

knee. (The weight is on the right foot.) This is the third count. Step the left foot next to the right to return to the beginning position for the fourth count. This is one set of Heel Tilts. Press both arms down and back as the heels touch forward, and return to slight abduction at the sides of the body as the feet step together. To increase the abdominal work, press both arms forward (as in Safe Arms) as the heels touch forward. The Heel Tilt works abdominals and tibialis anterior. Fast Heel Tilts are done by leaving out counts 2 and 4, and touching the left heel out as the right heel returns. During fast Heel Tilts, punch the left arm forward through the water as the right heel touches forward, and punch the right arms forward as the left heel touches.

Heel Turns

Begin with the feet in stride position. To do Heel Turns right: Touch the heel of the right foot to the pool bottom, with the toes pointed to the right (external hip rotation). This is the first count. Touch the toes of the right foot to the pool bottom, with the heel pointed to the right (internal hip rotation). This is the second count. Touch the heel of the right foot to the pool bottom, with the toes pointed to the right (external hip rotation). This is the third count. Bounce both feet together for the fourth count. This is one-half set of Heel Turns. To do Heel Turns left: Touch the heel of the left foot to the pool bottom, with the toes pointed to the left (external hip rotation). This is the first count. Touch the toes of the left foot to the pool bottom, with the heel pointed to the left (internal hip rotation). This is the second count. Touch the heel of the left foot to the pool bottom, with the toes pointed to the left (external hip rotation). This is the third count. Bounce both feet together for the fourth count. This is one full set of Heel Turns.

Flag Arms work well with Heel Turns (with the right forearm coming up and the left forearm going down as the right heel touches, and the right forearm going down and the left forearm going up as the right toe touches for Heel Turns right; the left arm going up and the right arm going down as the

— Heel Turns (position 1)

— Heel Turns (position 2)

left heel touches, and the left arm going down and the right arm going up as the left toe touches for Heel Turns left). Heel Turns work the hip rotators, adductors, abductors, gastrocnemius, and tibialis anterior. They can be varied by using Heel Turn Doubles and Singles. Heel Turns right would be two heel touches and two toe touches, followed by the Heel Turns right described above. Heel Turns left would be two heel touches and two toe touches, followed by the Heel Turns left described above. They would be cued as "heel, heel, toe, toe, heel, toe, heel, bounce" or "out, out, in, in, out, in, out, bounce."

Hip Flexor Stretch

See Iliopsoas Stretch.

Hoedown

Begin in stride position, with hips externally rotated (toes and knees pointed out). Bounce once on the right foot, while pulling the left foot up behind the knee of the right leg. Bounce once on the left foot, while pulling the right foot up behind the

— Hoedown

left knee. This is one set of Hoedowns. Hoedown works the hamstrings and quadriceps. Swing both arms laterally to the right as the left foot pulls behind the right knee and to the left as the right foot moves. This move can be varied by doing two Hoedowns with the left foot before changing to the right foot; this is called Hoedown Doubles. Another variation, Hoedown in Three, includes one set of Hoedowns (left and right), two Hoedowns left, one set of Hoedowns (right and left), and then two Hoedowns right.

Hop

Begin with the feet in stride position, the body weight over the right foot, and the left heel lifted back (knee flexion). Jump forward on the right leg four times for the first four counts of this move. Reverse and hop forward four times on the left foot for the last four counts of the move. Hops can move laterally to the right or left or backward also. Increasing the distance covered during one hop increases the intensity of the move. Hops work the gastrocnemius, quadriceps, and hamstrings but are primarily used to increase aerobic effort.

Hopscotch

Begin by bouncing once in stride position. This is the first count. For the second count, bounce once on the right foot, while pulling the left heel up behind the right thigh. Bounce once in

– Hopscotch

stride position with both feet down for the third count. For the fourth count, bounce on the left foot, while pulling the right heel up behind the left thigh. This is one set of Hopscotch. This move works the quadriceps and hamstrings. Arms begin extended laterally. The right arm presses down through the water toward the left heel as it pulls up behind the right thigh. Arms return to the beginning position for the third count. For the fourth count, the left arm presses down through the water toward the right heel.

Iliopsoas (Hip Flexor) Stretch

Stand, facing the pool edge, holding the pool edge with the left hand for support. Reach behind the body with the right hand, and grasp the lower-right leg, near the ankle. Push the right hip forward by contracting the right gluteals. The knee

– Iliopsoas (Hip Flexor) Stretch (version 1)

– Iliopsoas (Hip Flexor) Stretch (version 2)

will point back about one inch. By pointing the toes up, this is also an anterior tibialis stretch. Another variation to stretch the iliopsoas is to stand in a gastrocnemius stretch position and move into a pelvic tilt. The heel of the back foot will lift off the pool bottom as the knee pushes forward during the pelvic tilt.

Jazzkick

Begin in stride position. With the hip extended, flex (bend) the right knee, pulling the heel back toward the buttocks. This is the first count. Extend (straighten) the right knee, and slightly flex (bend) the hip. This is the second count. Repeat with the left leg. This move works the quadriceps and hamstrings. It can be varied by kicking to the diagonal (with the hips externally rotated) or kicking several times with one leg before switching to the other. Jog Arms work with Jazzkick. Using both arms in an Armswing Forward Flex and Short Backstroke move also works well.

Jazzkick Diagonals

Begin with Jazzkicks forward, alternating the right and left feet. Externally rotate the hips while continuing the Jazzkicks, kicking to the right diagonal with the right foot and to the left diagonal with the left foot.

Jig

Begin with the weight on the left foot, and the right heel ex-

— Jazzkick (position 1)

— Jig (position 1)

— Jig (position 2)

— Jazzkick (position 2)

— Jig (position 3)

— Jig (position 4)

tended to the right and touching the pool bottom. Point the toes on the right foot to the right. Pull the right heel up in front of the left knee for the first count. Return to the beginning position for the second count. Pull the right heel up behind the left knee for the third count. Move to stride position (feet about shoulder width apart) for the fourth count. Repeat with the left leg alternating legs, or do sets of four with each leg. This move works the quadriceps and hamstrings. Adduct the left arm down through the water, in front of and behind the body toward the right heel as it comes up in front of and behind the left knee. The right arm adducts down through the water behind and then in front of the body (opposite the left arm).

Jog Arms

Hold the elbows in at the waist and the forearms down at sides (arm and elbow extension). Bring the right forearm up and forward (elbow flexion) while taking a step with the left foot. Return the right arm to the beginning position (elbow extension). Bring the left forearm up and forward (elbow flexion) while taking a step with the right foot. Jog Arms work the biceps and triceps.

Jog Doubles

Begin with the feet in stride position. Step forward on the right foot while lifting the left foot off the pool bottom for the first count. Bounce once on the right foot while keeping the left foot off the pool bottom for the second count. Step forward on the left foot while lifting the right foot off the pool bottom for the third count. Bounce once on the left foot while keeping the right foot off the pool bottom for the fourth count. This is one set of Jog Doubles. Jog Doubles can be done in place or moving forward and backward. They work the gastrocnemius.

Jog Tilt

Lean the entire body slightly forward, keeping it straight (eliminate any spinal flexion that causes a bend at the waist), and jog forward. Lean the entire body slightly backward, keeping it straight, and jog backward. The degree of tilt in the body should be extremely small. This move works iliopsoas, gluteals, and abdominals. Jog Arms or Tricep Extensions and Backstroke arms work well with the Jog Tilt.

Jump Bounce

Begin in a closed stride position. Jump forward as far as possible, making a big jump for the first count. Do a small bounce in place for the second count. Together, this is one Jump Bounce forward. Jump backward (again, a big jump covering as much distance as possible) for the first count of a Jump Bounce back. Do a small bounce in place for the second count. Jump Bounces can be done singly, with one moving forward and one moving backward, or in series with four or eight each way. Safe Arms, pushing back in the Jump Bounce forward and forward in

— Jog Tilt (position 1)

— Jog Tilt (position 2)

the Jump Bounce backward, work well with this move. If done slowly, increase intensity by tucking the knees to the chest during the big jump (count 1). The Jump Bounce works iliopsoas, gluteals, and gastrocnemius but is usually used for increasing aerobic training.

Jumping Jack

Begin with the feet in stride position. Jump up and push both feet out to the sides into a wide stride position. Jump up again and bring both feet together. This is one Jumping Jack. Arms can be pressed down behind, in front, or with elbows flexed or out of the water, pushing up or flying out and up. Jumping Jacks can be done "in three" by jumping out, in, out, out and then in, out, in, in. They can also be done moving forward and backward or right and left to vary the intensity. Jumping Jacks work the adductors and abductors.

Jumping Jack Crossing

Begin with the feet in stride position. Jump up and push both feet out to the sides into a wide stride position. Jump up again and bring both feet together, with the right foot crossed over (in front and to the left of) the left foot. Jump "out" again, and then jump "in," with the left foot crossed over (in front and to the right of) the right foot. This is one set of Jumping Jack Crossing. Press the arms down, with one arm in

front of the body and one behind. The left arm should press in front of the body when the right foot crosses over the left, and the right arm should press in front of the body when the left foot crosses over the right. This move works adductors, abductors, deltoids, and latissimus dorsi.

— Jumping Jack Crossing (position 1)

— Jumping Jack Crossing (position 2)

Jumping Jack Doubles

Begin with the feet in stride position. Jump up and push both feet out to the sides into a wide stride position for the first count. Bounce once with both feet in the wide stride position for the second count. Jump up and bring both feet together for the third count. Bounce once with both feet together for the fourth count. This is one set of Jumping Jack Doubles. The Jumping Jack Doubles can be varied by moving forward and backward or right and left or by pulling both knees up (in the position they're in) between each count. This move works adductors and abductors. (See Jumping Jack for arm variations.)

Jumping Jack Jump

This move is sometimes called Split Jumps. Begin with the feet together. Jump high, moving both feet out to sides and

— Jumping Jack Jump

then back together; land with the feet together (beginning position). This is one Jumping Jack Jump. Any arm movements that help to maintain proper body alignment can be used. Arm movements that follow the legs out and in (a reverse press down) work well. Jumps works adductors and abductors and should be used only with well-conditioned students.

Karate Punch

Begin with the elbows in, toward the waist, flexed at about a 90-degree angle, forearms forward. Make fists. Punch the right arm across to the left until it is extended. While pulling the right elbow back to the beginning position, punch the left arm forward until it is extended. Continue punching alternate arms to a count of 1-2, 1-2. Reverse by punching the left arm across to the right and the

right arm forward. Feet, knees, and hips should pivot to the left when the right arm is punching to the left and pivot to the right when the left arm is punching to the right. When punching forward, the feet should be in the forward stride position. Bounce from one position to the next, or simply pivot easily on the balls of the feet. This move works the pectorals, deltoids, biceps, triceps, trapezius, and rhomboids.

Kick

Begin with the feet in stride position. Lift the right leg (hip flexion) forward, and then return it to the beginning position (hip extension). Repeat the two movements with the left leg. Kicks can be done quickly, lifting one leg while lowering the other, or they can be done slowly, bouncing both feet together before doing the next

kick. Maintain proper body alignment during Kicks, keeping the shoulders slightly back and the torso tall. Students will want to lean forward to kick higher. This should be discouraged. This move works the iliopsoas and gluteals.

Kick Corner

This move is sometimes called Kick Diagonal. Begin with the feet in stride position, with hips slightly externally rotated. Lift the right leg to the right diagonal, and return it to the beginning position. Repeat with the left leg. As with forward Kicks, Kick Corners can be done slowly or quickly. The same precautions apply. Kick Corners work the iliopsoas and gluteals.

Kick Point and Flex

Begin with the feet in stride position. Kick four or eight times, with the toes pointed forward (plantar flexed). Then kick forward the same amount of times with the toes pointed up toward the body (dorsi flexed). The kicks can be done slowly or quickly (as described in Kick) or forward or diagonally. This move works the gastrocnemius, anterior tibialis, iliopsoas, and gluteals.

Kickswing

Begin with the feet in stride position. Kick the right foot forward (hip flexion) as high as possible for the first count. Swing the right leg back into slight hip hyperextension (just

— Karate Punch (position 1)

— Karate Punch (position 2)

▬ Kick and Point

▬ Kick and Flex

past returning to beginning position) while bouncing once on the left leg for the second count. This is one Kickswing right. Repeat counts 1 and 2 three more times. Switch and do Kickswing left four times. To protect the lower back, contract the abdominals and hold the body in a pelvic tilt during the

swing portion of the move. For the Kickswing right, swing the right arm back and the left arm forward as the right leg kicks forward. Swing the right arm forward and the left arm back as the left leg kicks back. Reverse for the Kickswing left. The Kickswing works the iliopsoas and gluteals.

Kneelift

Begin with the feet in stride position. Lift the right leg (hip flexion) to approximately a 90-degree angle while bending the right knee (knee flexion) to the same angle. Repeat with the left leg. Kneelifts can be done quickly, lifting one leg while lowering the other (very much like a jog with high-lifting knees) or slowly, bouncing both feet together before doing the next Kneelift. Kneelifts can alternate right and left, doing single movements or repeating the movement two, four, or eight times on each leg. Kneelifts can be moving to the right and left to increase the intensity. Kneelifts work the iliopsoas and gluteals.

Kneelift Cross

Begin with the feet in stride position, with the right hip slightly internally rotated (toes and knees pointed in). Pull the right knee up toward the left shoulder, without allowing the shoulders to move forward. Return the right leg to the beginning position; repeat one, three, or seven more times. Repeat with the left leg. Touch the left

▬ Kneelift Cross

wrist to the inside (internal aspect) of the right knee and reverse. Trying to touch the left elbow to the right knee can result in simultaneous flexion and rotation of the spine, which may cause injury. Touching the wrist to the elbow allows the spine to stay erect (extended) while the spinal rotation occurs. Kneelift Crosses work the iliopsoas, gluteals, abductors, and adductors.

Kneelift Out

Begin with the feet in stride position, with both hips externally rotated (knees and toes pointed out). Pull the right knee up to the right diagonal, while keeping the torso tall (not tilting to the left), and bring it back down. Repeat with the left leg. Push both arms down in front or behind. Kneelifts Out (also called Open Kneelifts) can be

– Kneelift Out

done slowly or quickly or in groups of two, four, or eight (as described in Kneelifts). This move works the iliopsoas and gluteals.

Kneeswing Combo

This is a combination of the Kneeswing Up and Back and the Kneeswing Crossing. Do one set of Kneeswing Up and Back (swing the right knee up, back, and up, and then set the right foot down; swing the left knee up, back, and up, and then set the left foot down). Follow that with one set of Kneeswing Crossing (right knee crosses, opens, and crosses, and then set the right foot down; left knee crosses, opens, and crosses, and then set the left foot down). This is one set of Kneeswing Combo. Kneeswings can be also be combined by doing Kneeswing Up and Back four times

with the right leg and then four times with the left, followed by Kneeswing Crossing four times with the right leg and then four times with the left. They can also be combined doing two Kneeswings Up and Back and two Kneeswing Crossings with the right leg and then repeating with the left leg.

Kneeswing Crossing

Begin with the right knee flexed to a 90-degree angle (knee bent) and the right hip flexed to a 90-degree angle so the knee is pointing forward and the lower leg is straight down. The weight is on the left foot. Cross the right knee to the left (internally rotate the hip), while maintaining hip and knee flexion. This is the first count. Swing the knee out to the right side (externally rotate the hip), while maintaining hip and knee flexion. This is the second count.

Push both arms to the right as the knee crosses to the left, and push to the left as the knee swings out to the right. Kneeswing Crossings can be done in groups of two, four, or eight with the right leg before repeating with the left leg. Kneeswing Crossings work the hip abductors and adductors.

Kneeswing Diagonal

This a Kneeswing Up and Back with the hip slightly rotated externally so that the knee is pointed to the diagonal.

Kneeswing Up and Back

Begin with the right knee flexed to a 90-degree angle (knee bent) and the hip extended so the knee is pointing straight down. The weight is on the left foot. Swing the right knee forward, keeping it flexed at a 90-degree angle. This is the first count. Swing the right knee back

– Kneeswing Crossing (position 1)

– Kneeswing Crossing (position 2)

— Kneeswing Up and Back (position 1)

— Kneeswing Up and Back (position 2)

(while maintaining the knee flexion) to a slight hip hyperextension. This is the second count. Swing the left arm forward and backward with the right knee. Kneeswings with the right leg can be repeated one, three, or seven times more

before changing to the left. Move forward and backward to increase the intensity. This move works the iliopsoas and gluteals.

Lateral Push

Extend the right arm laterally to the right, palm down (pronated). The left arm begins adducted across the body, so that the left hand is about parallel with the right elbow; the palm of the left hand faces down (pronated) also. Hold both arms just below the water surface. To accomplish the Lateral Push, press both arms down slightly and to the left, just below the water surface. Reverse to move in the opposite direction. Arms push to the left when the body is moving right. This is an excellent move to use when moving laterally through the water. The Lateral Push works

— Lateral Push

the deltoids, latissimus dorsi, trapezius, and pectorals.

Leap Forward

Begin with the arms forward, just below the water surface, with palms out and knuckles almost touching. Kick the right

— Leap Forward (position 1)

— Leap Forward (position 2)

foot forward and jump forward onto it as the arms push out and back. Bring the left foot next to the right, while bringing the arms forward again. Repeat the leap with the right foot leading three more times, and then repeat it four times with the left foot leading. Jog or bounce backward to return to the beginning position. If the pool does not allow enough space to do four forward leaps with the right foot and then the left foot, leap two forward with the right foot and two forward with the left or leap four forward with the right foot leading, turn a half-turn left, and return with the left foot leading. This move works the iliopsoas, pectorals, trapezius, and gluteals.

Leap Side

Begin with the weight on the left foot, both arms extended to the right side and the right leg slightly lifted out to the side (abducted). Leap with the right leg to the right as far as possible while still facing forward and with both arms pushing down and to the left. This is the first count. Bring the left foot (adduct) next to the right, and bounce with both feet together. The arms should return to the beginning position. This is the second count. Repeat counts 1 and 2 three more times while moving to the right. To reverse the leap, begin with the left leg jumping out to the left and move left. Extend both arms to the left, and push down and to the

— Leap Side (position 1)

— Leap Side (position 2)

right during the jump for the first count. Leap Side works adductors and abductors. The toes of both feet should continually face forward, not to the sides, to ensure this. Leading the step with the heel will help to ensure proper forward alignment of the hips. Leap Side can be modified to work obliques by tightening the hips with the legs in the leap position, con-

centrating on moving from the waist, and keeping the upper torso stable.

Lift Hips

Begin with the back to the pool edge, the elbows up on the pool edge, the hips flexed at 90 degrees so that the knees are pointing forward, and the knees flexed at 90 degrees so that the feet are hanging down. The back must be flat to the pool wall. Slowly contract the abdominal muscles so that the knees move forward an inch or two. This will move the very lower back and hips away from the pool edge. Return the back to the beginning position without allowing the midback to move away from the pool wall. This move works the abdominals. If done incorrectly, with the knees moving up and down rather than forward and backward, it will work the iliopsoas muscles. If the hip joint is moving (flexing and extending), form is incorrect. If the spine is moving, form is correct, and the abdominals will be working. This move can be modified by changing the flexion in the knees and hips.

— Lift Hips

Mule Kick

Begin with the feet in stride position. Flex (bend) the right knee, while maintaining hip extension (a straight line down from the hip to the knee) in the right leg. This is the first count. Extend (straighten) the right knee, and return to beginning position for the second count. This is a Mule Kick right. Repeat with the left leg for Mule Kick left (counts 3 and 4). Mule Kicks are simple knee flexion (trying to kick the heel up to the buttocks) while keeping the knee pointed straight down (hip flexors extended). Mule Kicks can be done alternating right and then left, or four to eight can be done with the right leg before changing to the left. Mule Kicks can be done quickly (without a bounce between each kick) or slowly (with a bounce between each kick). Mule Kicks work the quadriceps and ham-

strings. Optional arm movements include Elbow Press and Scissor Arms. Two other arm variations are as follows:

1. Begin with the elbows flexed at about a 90-degree angle and pulled into the waist, with forearms forward. Lift both elbows laterally as the heel kicks behind, and lower them as the foot returns. This can also be done with the arms beginning straight down at the sides of the body.
2. Begin with the arms down in front of body, with the palms on the thighs; make fists. Lift both arms forward as the heel kicks behind, and lower them as the foot returns.

Neck Stretch

Tilt the head to the right side, moving the right ear to the right shoulder. Reverse for Neck Stretch left.

Oblique Stretch

Stand with the feet shoulder width apart, the toes pointed slightly out and the knees slightly bent. Put the left hand on the left hip, and extend the right arm up and over the head without moving the toes or knees. This should stretch the obliques. If further stretch is required, slowly bend sideways toward the hand on the hip.

— Oblique Stretch

Over and Present

Begin with the arms extended laterally (out to the sides), just beneath the water surface, palms forward. With the elbow extended so the arm is straight, bring the right hand toward the left until they are almost touching. Turn the palm out (externally rotate), and push the extended right arm back to the beginning position. This can

— Mule Kick

— Neck Stretch

— Over and Present (position 1)

— Over and Present (position 2)

knee. To work the obliques, stand with the feet shoulder width apart, and move only from the waist up. The knees should be slightly flexed, and both knees and toes should point slightly out.

Paddlekick

This move is done in a floating position, with the back to the pool edge and the elbows on the pool edge. Hold a milk jug in each hand or a kickboard under each arm. With the hips and knees flexed (bent) at a 90-degree angle (so the knees don't point forward and the feet hang down), alternately extend each knee, keeping both knees on the same plane. This move works the quadriceps and hamstrings.

Pectoral Stretch

Interlace the fingers behind the head, with the elbows pointed out to the sides. Squeeze the

shoulder blades together. See also Bicep, Anterior Deltoid, and Pectoral Stretch.

Pelvic Tilt

Begin by standing in a comfortable upright position. Create an anterior pelvic tilt by using one or more of these imagery techniques:

- Pull the navel back to the spine.
- Press the stomach down toward the pool bottom.
- Tuck the buttocks under.
- Take the arch out of the lower back.

Doing any of these is one pelvic tilt. The pelvic tilt can be used during many exercise moves to protect the lower back from strain. A series of 8 to 24 standing pelvic tilts can be used during the toning portion of the workout. The pelvic tilt works the abdominal muscles.

be repeated with the right arm several times before switching to the left, or it can be done alternating right and left. This works the pectorals, anterior serratus, trapezius, rhomboids, and lattisimus dorsi. To maintain integrity of the knee joint, pivot each foot to follow the

— Pectoral Stretch

— Pelvic Tilt

Press Down Behind

Begin with the arms laterally extended (lifted to the sides), just beneath the water surface, with palms down (pronated). Push both arms down through the water until they almost meet behind the body. This portion of the move focuses on the latissimus dorsi and trapezius. To reverse, simply keep the palms down and lift the arms with force through the water to the beginning position. This portion of the move focuses on the deltoids. When used for toning, pause momentarily between the initial and reverse portions of the move.

– Press Down Behind

Press Down Front

Begin with the arms extended laterally (lifted out to the sides), just beneath the water surface, with palms down (pronated). Push both arms down through the water until they almost meet in front of the body. This

portion of the move focuses on the pectorals and serratus anterior. To reverse, simply keep the palms down and lift the arms with force through the water to the beginning position. This portion of the move focuses on the deltoids. When used for toning, pause momentarily between the initial and reverse portions of the move.

Press Down Singles

Begin with the arms extended laterally (lifted out to the sides), just beneath the water surface, with palms down (pronated). At the same time, press the right arm down (as described in Press Down Front) and the left arm down (as described in Press Down Behind). Reverse the move (also as described). To continue, press the left arm down in front and the right arm down behind, and lift them both to the beginning position. This is one set of Press Down Singles. The deltoids, pectorals, serratus anterior, latissimus dorsi, and trapezius are all involved in this move.

Press Down with Elbows Flexed

Begin with the elbows extended laterally (lifted out to the sides), the forearms forward (90 to 120 degree elbow flexion), and the palms down. The arms should begin just below the water surface. Push both arms down through the water until the forearms almost meet in front of the body. This portion of the move works the pectorals and serratus anterior. To reverse,

– Press Down with Elbows Flexed

lift the arms with force back to the beginning position. The reverse portion of the move works the deltoids and trapezius.

Quadricep Stretch

Stand, facing the pool edge. Hold the pool edge with the left hand for support. Reach behind the body with the right hand,

– Quadricep Stretch

and grasp the lower-right leg near the ankle. Pull the lower-right leg and heel gently toward the right buttocks. The knee and toes should point directly to the pool bottom, straight down. Reverse for the left Quadricep Stretch.

Reach Pull-In

Begin with both arms extended to the left at shoulder level, just

– Reach Pull-In (position 1)

– Reach Pull-In (position 2)

beneath the water surface. The feet, knees, hips, and shoulders pivot to the left to allow the palms to begin in a parallel position. This is the "Reach" position of this move. While pivoting the feet, knees, and hips forward, pull both elbows back until the shoulder blades are squeezed together. This is the "Pull-In" portion of the move. Continue to the left before switching to the right, or alternate by doing one left and then one right. It can be done bouncing into the pivot and back to the forward position or simply pivoting lightly with no bounce. Reach Pull-In involves the pectorals, deltoids, trapezius, and rhomboids.

Reverse Crossing Jog

Begin with the feet in stride position. Reverse Crossing Jog moves laterally to the right with four or eight steps before moving laterally to the left with four or eight steps. To do the move to the right: Step the right foot laterally to the right, shifting the weight to the right foot while lifting the left leg up slightly, off the pool bottom. This is the first count. Step the left foot behind the right foot, shifting the weight to the left foot while lifting the right foot up slightly for the second count. Repeat counts 1 and 2 three to seven times while moving to the right. To do the move to the left: Step the left foot laterally to the left, shifting the weight to the left foot while lifting the right foot up slightly, off the

– Reverse Crossing Jog (position 1)

– Reverse Crossing Jog (position 2)

pool bottom. This is the first count. Step the right foot behind the left foot, shifting the weight to the right foot while lifting the left foot up slightly. This is the second count. Repeat counts 1 and 2 three to seven times while moving to the left. In both Reverse Crossing Jog left and right, the arms can stay on the hips or push laterally to the right (when moving left) or left (when moving right). Keep the torso facing forward to achieve the excellent oblique, adductor, and abductor work the Reverse Crossing Jog provides. This jog can also be done with the leading foot crossing behind instead of in front as described above. While moving left, the right foot would step behind the left foot for the first count of each two-count segment. While moving right, the left foot would step behind the right foot during the first count of each two-count segment. This is called Crossing Jog Behind; it also works the adductors and abductors. The Crossing Jog done in front and behind can be combined to create a grapevine move. A two-count segment of Crossing Jog in front moving left would be followed by a two-count segment behind moving left; repeat twice before reversing to the right. This can be called a Crossing Jog Combo or Grapevine. The cues would be "cross, step, back, step, cross, step, back, step."

Rhomboid Stretch

Place the palms on center of the upper back and press elbows together.

Rock in Three

Begin with the weight on the left foot, and lift the right foot slightly out to the right side (abducted). This is the first

- **Rhomboid Stretch**

count. For the second count, step the right foot down, and lift the left foot slightly out to the left side (adducted). Step the left foot down and lift the right foot out to the right side (beginning position) for the third count. For the fourth count, pivot slightly to the right on the left foot, and kick the right leg to the right. Step the right foot down and lift the left foot out to the left side for the fifth count. Step the left foot down and lift the right foot out to the right side (beginning position) for the sixth count. Step the right foot down and lift the left foot out to the left side for the seventh count. For the eighth count, pivot slightly to the left on the right foot, and kick the left leg to the left. This is one set of Rock in Three. This move works the adductors, abductors, iliopsoas, and gluteals.

Rock Side to Side

Begin with the weight on the left foot, and lift the right foot slightly out to the right side (abducted). Step the right foot down, and lift the left foot slightly out to the left side (adducted). This is one set of Rock Side to Side. Arm movements can include Press Downs alternately or Lateral Pushes to the left (as the right leg rocks out) and right (as the left leg rocks out). The Rock Side to Side works the adductors and abductors. Lead the rocking with the heel to help keep the toes of both feet pointing forward continually and the hips in forward alignment. The Rock Side to Side can be modified to work the obliques by tightening the hip joints (with the legs in a rocking position) and concentrating on moving from the waist and keeping the upper body stable.

- **Rock Side to Side**

Rocking Horse

Begin with the weight on the left foot, and lift the right foot slightly in front of the body (hip flexion). Step the right foot forward. Lean the body forward over the right foot, keeping the body straight. Avoid any spinal flexion that might cause the body to bend at the waist. Lift

— Rocking Horse (position 1)

— Rocking Horse (position 2)

the left foot up off the pool bottom, and kick slightly back as the weight shifts to the right foot. This is the first count of Rocking Horse. Step the left foot back to the beginning position, and lean the body slightly back over the left foot, keeping the body straight. Avoid any spinal hyperextension that might cause the body to bend backward at the waist. Lift the right foot up off the pool bottom, and kick slightly forward as the weight shifts to the left foot. This is the second count of Rocking Horse. Repeat counts 1 and 2 three more times. Then switch to Rocking Horse left, with the left foot rocking forward and the right foot rocking backward. The Rocking Horse works the iliopsoas, gluteals, and abdominals. Safe Arms, pushing back as the body leans (rocks) forward and pushing forward as the body rocks backward, works well with this move (see Safe Arms).

This move can be varied by doing it to the right and left diagonals rather than forward. This is called Rocking Horse Diagonals. Lift the right leg toward the right diagonal and turn the body in that direction before stepping on the right foot for the first count. Lift the left leg toward the left diagonal and turn the body in that direction before stepping on the left foot for the second count.

Rocking Horse Doubles

Rock forward on the right foot (as described in Rocking Horse)

for the first count. Bounce once on the right foot (keeping it in first-count position) for the second count. Rock back on the left foot (as described in Rocking Horse) for the third count. Bounce once on the left foot (keeping it in the third-count position) for the fourth count. This is one set of Rocking Horse Doubles right. Repeat counts 1 through 4 three more times before switching to Rocking Horse Doubles left (with the left foot rocking forward and bouncing and then the right foot rocking back and bouncing). The Rocking Horse Doubles work the iliopsoas, gluteals, and abdominals. Safe Arms works well with this move. This move can also be varied by rocking to the diagonals.

Rocking Horse in Three

Rock forward on the right foot (as described in Rocking Horse) for the first count. Rock back on the left foot (as described in Rocking Horse) for the second count. Rock forward on the right foot to return to the first-count position. Kick the left foot forward as the body returns to an upright position for the fourth count. (This much of the move is called Rocking Horse in Three right.) Rock forward on the left foot for the fifth count, backward on the right for the sixth count, and forward on the left for the seventh count. Kick the right foot forward as the body returns to an upright position for the eighth count. (This portion of the move is called Rocking Horse in Three left.) The combination of everything done so far is one set of Rocking Horse in Three. This move works the iliopsoas, gluteals, and abdominals. Safe Arms works well with this move.

This move can be combined with Rocking Horse Doubles for a move called Rocking Horse Three and Doubles. Do a Rocking Horse in Three right, a Rocking Horse Doubles left, a Rocking Horse in Three left, and a Rocking Horse Doubles right. This is one set of Rocking Horse Three and Doubles. Students can learn well with these cues on the beats: "up, back, up, kick, up, up, back, back" (repeat these words twice for one full set of Rocking Horse Three and Doubles) **or** "right, left, right, kick, left, left, right, right; left, right, left, kick, right, right, left, left." These moves can also be varied by using Rocking Horse Diagonals.

Rocking Horse Seven and Up

Rock forward on the right foot (as described in Rocking Horse) for the first count. Rock back on the left foot (as described in Rocking Horse) for the second count. Rock forward on the right foot for the third count, backward on the left foot for the fourth count, forward on the right foot for the fifth count, backward on the left foot for the sixth count, and forward on the right foot for the seventh count. Kick the left foot forward for the eighth count. This portion of the move is called Rocking

Horse Seven and Up right. Rock forward on the right foot, backward on the left, forward on the right, backward on the left, forward on the right, backward on the left, forward on the right (counts 1–7); then kick the right foot forward for count 8. This is Rocking Horse Seven and Up left. This entire move is one set of Rocking Horse Seven and Up. This move works the iliopsoas, gluteals, and abdominals. Safe Arms works well with this move.

The Rocking Horse Seven and Up can be combined with Rocking Horse Doubles for variety; it's called Rocking Horse Seven and Doubles. Do one set of Rocking Horse Seven and Up right for the first eight counts, two sets of Rocking Horse Doubles left for the second eight counts, one set of Rocking Horse Seven and Up left for the third eight counts, and two sets of Rocking Horse Doubles right for the fourth eight counts. This is one set of Rocking Horse Seven and Doubles. These can also be varied by using Rocking Horse Diagonals.

Russian Kick

This move must be done in shallow water to be accomplished successfully. With the hips and knees flexed (bent) as much as possible (almost sitting in the pool), alternately extend each knee without changing the degree of hip flexion. The arms can be held in a folded position in front of chest, like Russian dancers do, or they can punch alternately in opposition to the

— Russian Kick

kicks. Russian Kicks work quadriceps, hamstrings, and gluteals.

Safe Arms

Begin with the arms extended out to the sides, just beneath the water surface, with the palms forward. With the elbows

— Safe Arms

extended so the arms are straight, bring the hands together in front of the body. Turn the palms back, and with straight arms, bring the hands together (or as close as possible) behind the body. This move works the pectorals, anterior serratus, trapezius, rhomboids, and lattisimus dorsi. Rocking Horses and Forward and Back Lunges work well with Safe Arms.

Scissor Arms

Begin with the arms extended laterally, palms down. With the elbows extended so the arms are straight, push the arms straight down in front of the body until the palms meet. With the shoulders back and palms still down, pull the arms up with force to the beginning position. This move can be varied by crossing the hands in the lowered position in front of the body, increasing the range of motion involved in the movement. The serratus anterior, pectorals, lattisimus dorsi, deltoids, and trapezius are all involved in this move. Scissor Arms can be used in Jumping Jacks and most lateral movements, such as Side Step and Side Kick.

Scissors

Begin standing, with the feet together. Bounce into a cross-country ski position, with the right foot at least 12 inches in front of the left. Bounce into the reverse position, with the left foot in front of the right. When the right foot is forward, swing or punch the left arm forward and then reverse. This move can be varied by pointing the toes of the forward foot up (dorsi flexed) while tilting the body slightly back. It can also be varied by pointing the toes of the back foot down while tilting the body slightly forward. Scissors can be done moving forward, backward, or in a circle to increase the intensity. Scissors work the iliopsoas and gluteals. Tilting backward with the toes of the front foot dorsi flexed focuses work on the iliopsoas and also involves the tibialis anterior and abdominals. Tilting forward with the toes of the back foot down focuses work on the gluteals and involves the gastrocnemius.

Scissors Jump

Begin standing, with the feet together. This move is sometimes called Vertical Jump. Jump into a cross-country ski position, with the right foot in front of the left. While still suspended in the water, bring both

— **Scissor Arms**

— **Scissors**

— **Scissors Jump**

feet together, and land with them next to each other. Jump into a cross-country ski position, with the left foot in front of the right. While still suspended in the water, bring both feet together, and land with them next to each other. Scissors Jumps work the iliopsoas, gluteals, and gastrocnemius. The left arm should swing forward as the right leg goes forward and vice versa. Scissors Jumps should be used in high-intensity classes for well-conditioned students only.

Scissors Turn

Begin standing, with the feet together. Bounce into a cross-country ski position, with the right foot about 12 inches in front of the left. This is count 1. For the second count, pivot (or bounce) a half turn to the left, keeping the feet in the same place but changing their position so that the body faces the back of the pool. Bounce twice with the feet together for counts 3 and 4. Repeat counts 1 through 4 to return facing the front. The Scissors Turn works the iliopsoas, gluteals, gastrocnemius, and obliques. It can be done with quarter turns rather than half turns. Bounce into the cross-country ski position (as stated above) for count one. For count 2, pivot or bounce a quarter turn to the left. Bounce twice with the feet together for counts 3 and 4. To face each wall with this move, repeat counts 1 through 4 four times.

Scissors with Bounce

Begin standing, with the feet together. Bounce into a cross-country ski position, with the right foot about 12 inches in front of the left. Bounce, bringing both feet together again. Bounce into a cross-country ski position, with the left foot about 12 inches in front of the right. Bounce, bringing both feet together again. The arm movements and variations written for Scissors also apply to Scissors with Bounce. The Scissors with Bounce can also be varied by twisting the body so the toes of the right foot point to the right diagonal when the right foot is forward and the toes of the left foot point to the left diagonal when the left foot is forward. This move works the iliopsoas and gluteals.

Scrunch

Buoyant bells, balls, or jugs are needed. Begin in a supine position (lying on back); flex the knees and hips. Round the shoulders forward, and "scrunch" them to the knees. Do not extend to a straight leg position. The Scrunch works the abdominal muscles.

Shoulder Shrug

Standing in stride position (with feet shoulder width apart), arms relaxed at the sides, squeeze the shoulders together in front of the body. Then squeeze the shoulders together behind the body. Shoulder Shrugs work the pectorals, deltoids, trapezius, and rhomboids.

They can be done with moves like Jumping Jacks or alone for joint lubrication during the warm-up.

Side Circle

Begin standing at the pool edge, holding the pool edge to stabilize the body. The weight is on the left foot, with the right leg straight down and the right foot next to the left foot. Extend the right leg back (hip hyperextension), and circle it out to the side, around to the front, and back to the beginning position. Repeat seven more times and then reverse. During the reverse, the right leg will move forward (hip flexion), circle out to the side, and around to the back before returning to the beginning position. Repeat the Side Circles back and forward with the left leg. As the leg circles, the body should remain in good alignment. If the upper body moves around, the leg circles should be smaller. The Side Circles work adductors, abductors, iliopsoas, and gluteals. This is a toning move and should not be used during the aerobic portion of the workout.

Side Lift

The Side Lift is a toning move. It is a Side Kick done without the bounce (see Side Kick).

Side Lift Flex

This is a Side Kick with the knee slightly flexed. It is used during the toning portion of the workout. Hold onto the pool

– Side Lift Flex

– Side Press

times to the left; step the left foot out to the left, and move the right foot next to the left foot's new position. The arms can be kept straight, or the elbows can be flexed up to a 90 degree angle. Straight or slightly flexed arms will provide the highest intensity. Complete flexion will provide the the lowest intensity. The Side Step works the abductors, adductors, deltoids, and lattisimus dorsi.

Side Touch

See Touch Side.

Side Train

Begin with the feet together. For the first count, step the right foot out to the right side, and shift the body weight to that leg by lifting the left foot up from the beginning position. For the second count, step the left foot back to the beginning position, and shift the body weight to that leg by lifting the right foot up. Step the right foot back to the beginning position for the third count, and shift the body weight to that leg by lifting the left foot up from the beginning position. For the fourth count, step the left foot back to the beginning position. This is one Side Train right. Repeat counts 1 through 4 three or seven more times. Reverse to do four or eight Side Trains left. Lateral Pushes to the left (as the right foot steps right during the Side Train right) and right (as the left foot steps left during the Side Train left) can be used.

edge for stability. With the knee pointing straight down (hip extension) and flexed to about a 120-degree angle, do 8 to 16 Side Kicks with no bounce. The upper body should be upright and stable. Shorten the range of motion in the leg if the upper body moves. The knee flexion will increase the water's drag on the leg and thus enhance the toning benefits. The knee joint should be consciously tightened to avoid torque. The Side Lift Flex works the abductors and adductors.

Side Press

The Side Press is a variation of the Tricep Extension (see Tricep Extension). For Side Press Out, begin with the hands on the hips and the elbows out to the side. Turn the palms away from the body (pronate), and press the forearms out to the sides

(extend elbows). For Side Press In, return to the beginning position from the extended Side Press Out. The Press In concentrates on biceps, while the Press Out concentrates on triceps.

Side Step

Begin with the feet together and the arms at the sides. For the first count, step the right foot out to the right (keep the toes pointed forward and allow the knees to bend), and lift both arms out to the sides (a reverse Press Down). Shift the body weight to the right foot, and move the left foot next to the right foot's new position as arms lower for the second count. The body will be in the beginning position but two to three feet to the right of the actual starting place. Repeat counts 1 and 2 three more times, moving to the right. Then Side Step four

━ Side Train (position 1)

━ Side Train (position 2)

━ Side Train (position 3)

━ Side Train (position 4)

Repeat the move to the left for a Sidebend left. The Sidebend works the obliques. Be careful to bend to the *side* only, not forward or backward during the Sidebend. This is a much smaller move than participants expect it to be. Emphasize the small range of motion that will be experienced.

Sidekick

Begin in stride position. Lift the right leg out to the side (abduct) while bouncing once on the left leg for the first count. Return the right leg to the beginning position (adduct), and bounce on both feet for the second count. Abduct the left leg while bouncing once on the right leg for the third count; adduct the left leg to the beginning position, and bounce on both feet for the fourth count. This is one set of Sidekicks. Properly

━ Sidekick

A reverse Press Down, with the elbows flexed or the arms straight, can also be used (with the lift coming during the step to the right during the Side Train right and during the step to the left during the Side Train left). The Side Train works abductors and adductors.

Sidebend

Begin with the feet in stride position, knees slightly flexed, hips tucked under, and abdominals contracted. While bending sideways at the waist, tilt the upper torso toward the right (lateral spinal flexion right). This a Sidebend right.

position the leg, with the toes pointing forward and the heel pointing slightly out to the right, before kicking out to the right. The Sidekick can be varied by doing two, four, or eight with the right leg before switching to the left leg. Press Down Behind and Press Down Front arm moves both work well with the Sidekick. The Sidekick works the adductors and abductors.

Sidekick Forward and Backward

Begin in stride position. Lift the right leg out to the side (abduct), and bounce once on the left leg for the first count. Return the right leg (adduct) to just in front of the left ankle while bouncing once on the left leg for the second count. Abduct the right leg while bouncing once on the left leg for the third count. Adduct the right leg to just behind the left ankle while bouncing once on the left leg for the fourth count. This is one Sidekick Forward and Backward. If used during the toning portion of the workout, this move should be repeated four or eight times before switching to the left leg. If used during the aerobics portion, it should be done only once on the right leg before switching to the left leg. Also incorporate hand movements if used during the aerobics portion. Press Down the left arm in front of the body (and the right arm behind) when the right leg is adducted in front of the left

— Sidekick Forward

— Sidekick Backward

ankle, and Press Down the right arm in front of the body (and the left arm behind) when the left leg is adducted behind the right ankle. Sidekick Forward and Backward works the adductors and abductors.

Ski Bounce

Begin with the feet in stride position. Bounce, moving both feet together to the right and then to the left, as if schussing down a ski hill. This move works the quadriceps and hamstrings if done with concentration on flexing and extending the knees. It works obliques if done with concentration on the movement coming from the waist and keeping the upper torso stable. Tricep Extensions back work well with the Ski Bounce.

Slide

The Slide is a bouncing side-step, moving laterally to the right and then to the left. Begin in stride position for the Slide right: Step the right foot to the right side for the first count. Step the left leg next to the right, while lifting the right foot up off the pool bottom for the second count. Repeat counts 1 and 2 three to seven times moving to the right. For the Slide left: Step the left foot to the left for the first count. Step the right leg next to the left, while lifting the left leg up off the pool bottom for the second count. Repeat counts 1 and 2 three to seven times moving to the left. This is one full set of Slides. Press Down arm moves work well with the Slide. The Slide works the adductors and abductors.

Spider Crawl

Begin facing the pool edge, with the feet on the pool wall and the hands holding the gutter. Crawl or shuffle down the pool wall in one direction; then switch direction. The feet should remain in contact with the pool wall, and the hands should remain palms down on the edge of pool. The more frequently direction is changed, the higher the intensity of the move.

Stroke

Begin with the left hand on the left hip and the right hand extended laterally to the left, palm facing forward. Move the right hand just below the water surface, pushing to the right; push until the body has to pivot right as the right arm reaches slightly behind it on the right side. Repeat with the left arm beginning on the right, the palm catching the water and pushing it to the left. For a faster pace, shorten the range of motion. This move works the pectorals, deltoids, rhomboids, and trapezius.

◼ Stroke

Swing Twist

Begin with feet in stride position. Bounce both feet to turn the toes to the right for the first count (feet pivot but stay in place on pool bottom). This is a Swing Twist right. Bounce both feet (in place) to turn the toes to the left for the second count. This is a Swing Twist left. The entire move to both sides is one set of Swing Twists. During the Swing Twist right, push both arms to the left, and during the Swing Twist left, push the arms to the right. This move can be varied by moving forward and backward, right and left, or in a circle. The Swing Twist works the obliques.

◼ Swing Twist

Swing Twist Doubles

Begin with the feet in stride position. Bounce both feet to turn the toes to the right for the first count (feet pivot but stay

in place on pool bottom). Bounce once in that position for the second count. Bounce both feet (in place) to turn the toes to the left for the third count. Bounce once in that position for the fourth count. This is one set of Swing Twist Doubles. This move can be varied like the Swing Twist. It works the obliques.

Swing Twist in Three

Begin with one set of Swing Twists for counts 1 and 2. On counts 3 and 4, do Swing Twist Doubles right. On counts 5 and 6, do Swing Twists left and right. On counts 7 and 8, do Swing Twist Doubles left. The toes turn right, left, right, right, left, right, left, left. This move can be varied like the Swing Twist. It works the obliques.

Swing Twist with Back Toes Down (see photo at the top of the next page)

Begin doing a Swing Twist (as described in Swing Twist). During the Swing Twist right, point the toes of the back foot (left) down (plantar flex) toward the pool bottom. During the Swing Twist left, point the toes of the back foot (right) down toward the pool bottom. Pointing the back toes down during the Swing Twist adds gluteal work to the move, which ordinarily works the obliques. The "Toes Down" adaption can be used during Swing Twist, Swing Twist Doubles, and Swing Twist in Three.

— Swing Twist with Back Toes Down

Swing Twist with Front Toes Up

Begin doing a Swing Twist (as described in Swing Twist). During the Swing Twist right, point the toes of the front foot (right) up toward the body (dorsi flex). During the Swing Twist left, point the toes of the front foot (left) up toward the body. The Swing Twist with Front Toes Up works the obliques and tibialis anterior. The "Toes Up" adaption can be used during Swing Twist, Swing Twist Doubles, and Swing Twist in Three.

Swish

Begin in stride position, with the toes pointed slightly out (slight external hip rotation) and the arms extended laterally (abducted), just beneath the water surface. (The elbows are straight, and the arms are straight out to the sides.) Rotate the spine (twist) to the right, so that the right hand moves back about 6 to 12 inches and the left hand moves forward about 6 to 12 inches. Return to the beginning position. Then twist to the left, so the arms move 6 to 12 inches in the opposite direction. The body should not move from the hips down. Students will think this is an arm movement; it is not. The arms stay in place in relation to the torso. The movement comes from the waist, which causes the arms to move. Students who are unable to accomplish this move without moving the lower body should pivot to the right during the Swish right and vice versa. This will protect the knee joints. The Swish works the obliques.

Touch Back

Begin with the feet in stride position. Move the toes of the right foot backward on the pool bottom for the first count. Return to the beginning position for the second count. Move the

— Swing Twist with Front Toes Up

— Swish

— Touch Back

toes of the left foot backward on the pool bottom for the third count. Return the left foot to the beginning position for the fourth count. Swing the right arm forward and the left arm backward as the toes of the right foot touch back. Touch Backs can be done in series of four or eight with the right leg before changing to the left leg. They can also be done alternately (as described above) or in threes: right, left, right, right and left, right, left, left. Touch Backs work the gluteals and iliopsoas. They are sometimes called Back Touches.

Touch Forward

Begin with the feet in stride position. For the first count, move the toes of the right foot forward on the pool bottom. This will cause slight hip flexion. Swing the left arm forward and the right arm backward as the toes touch forward. Return to the beginning position for the second count. Repeat counts 1 and 2 using the left foot for counts 3 and 4. Touch Forwards can be done four or eight times with the right foot before changing to the left foot or alternately (as described above). Touch Forwards work the gluteals and iliopsoas. They are sometimes called Forward Touches.

Touch Side

Begin with the feet together. Move the toes of the right foot to the right side along the pool bottom for the first count. Return to the beginning position

for the second count. Move the toes of the left foot to the left side along the pool bottom for the third count. Return to the beginning position for the fourth count. This is one set of Touch Sides. Touch Sides can be done slowly with the feet bouncing together between each touch (as described above) or quickly in a rocking-type movement, with the right foot returning to beginning position as the left foot is touching to the left and vice versa. Armswing Sides work well with Touch Sides. This move can be done in a series or four or eight with the right foot before changing to the left foot. Touch Sides work the adductors and abductors. They are sometimes called Side Touches.

Touch-Up

Do a Touch Side with the right foot while bouncing once on the left foot for the first count (see Touch Side). Do a Kneelift Cross with the right foot while bouncing once on the left foot for the second count (see Kneelift Cross). Repeat counts 1 and 2 three times before changing to the left foot. Do a Touch Side with the left foot while bouncing once on the left foot for the first count. Do a Kneelift Cross with the left leg while bouncing once on the right foot for the second count. Repeat counts 1 and 2 three more times with the left foot. This is one full set of Touch-Ups. Since it is not recommended to bounce more than eight times successively

■ Touch-Up (position 1)

■ Touch-Up (position 2)

on one foot, do not do more than four Touch-Ups on one foot before changing to the other, unless weight is equally displaced between both legs during the Touch Side. Tricep Extensions pressing back as the knee comes up work well with Touch-Ups. Touch-Ups work the iliopsoas, gluteals, and abductors.

Trapezius Stretch

With the fingers interlaced in front of the body, arms at shoulder height, turn the palms outward as arms extend forward until a stretch is felt in the upper back. The trapezius can be stretched further by doing Neck Stretches to each side; then relax the chin and drop it down on the chest (see Neck Stretch). An alternative Trapezius Stretch can be done by placing both hands on either side of the neck. Tilt the head forward and down.

— Trapezius Stretch

— Tricep Extension Back

— Tricep Extension Out

— Tricep Extension Forward

Tricep Extension

This move is the reverse of the Bicep Curl but with the palms facing the other way (pronated) (see Bicep Curl). Tricep Extensions back begin with the elbows flexed at about a 90-degree angle. The forearms are down next to waist, and the elbows are about three to six inches back from the body. The arms (shoulders) are slightly hyperextended. In this position, press the forearms back through the water (elbow extension). Tricep Extensions out begin in the same position but with the palms facing out (away from the body). Press the forearms out through the water. Tricep Extensions forward begin with the elbows next to the waist and completely flexed. Extend the elbow or press the palms down to the outer thighs. These moves all work the triceps and biceps.

Tricep Stretch

With the arms overhead, hold the elbow of the right arm with the left hand. Gently pull the right elbow to the left behind the head, stretching the tricep. To increase the stretch, bend the elbow of the right arm. This also stretches the latissimus dorsi. Reverse for the left arm.

— Tricep Stretch

Tuck Jump

Begin with the feet in stride position and the arms extended laterally, just below the water surface. Pull both knees up to the chest while pressing the arms down through the water and under the knees. The ab-

— Tuck Jump

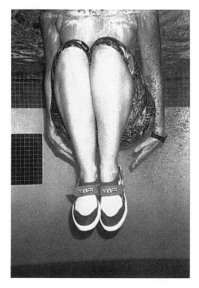

dominal muscles should be contracted. Tuck Jumps work iliopsoas and gluteals.

Twist

Begin with the feet in wide stride position, knees slightly flexed, hips tucked under, abdominals tightened, and ribs lifted. While keeping the toes, knees, and hips pointed forward, twist the upper torso toward the right (spinal rotation right). This is the first count. Return to the beginning position for the second count. Twist the torso to the left for the third count, and return to the beginning position for the fourth count. This is one set of Twist. It can be varied to protect the knee joints by pivoting the feet, knees, and hips in the same direction as the twist. The Twist works obliques.

Two-Step

The Two-Step is simply two Side Steps right followed by two Side Steps left (see Side Step).

Waist Curl

The Waist Curl is a Bicep Curl in which the elbows stay close to the waist (see Bicep Curl). It can be done forward, with the forearms forward moving up and down; in, with the forearms across the body moving up and down; and out, with the forearms out to the sides moving up and down. The palm always faces up (supinated). Waist Curls work the biceps and triceps.

Waterpull

Begin with both arms extended laterally to the left; then pull the elbows in toward the waist, palms facing forward. This is the beginning position. Push both arms through the water to the right and then to the left. The range of motion will be short because of the flexed position of the elbows. Lowering the arms deeper into the water and then bringing them back to the surface will increase the interest and intensity of this move. This move works the biceps and triceps but can be modified to work the pectorals, deltoids, rhomboids, and trapezius by extending the elbows. It is often done without any foot movement for upper-body toning, but Rock Side to Side can work well with it.

— Waterpull

Wind-Up and Present

Begin with the arms extended laterally, palms down. With the elbow extended so the arm is straight, press the right arm down in front of the body; continue moving it left and up until it is parallel with the left arm. This is the "Wind-Up" portion of the move. Turn the right palm out and push across, just below the water surface, to the beginning position. This is the "Present" portion of the move. Continue with several, using the right arm and then switching to the left, or alternate using the right and left arms. The pectorals, deltoids, trapezius, and rhomboids are all involved in Wind-Up and Present. To involve the obliques, keep the

— Wind-Up and Present (position 1)

— Wind-Up and Present (position 2)

lower body stationary with the feet in a wide stance, pointed slightly outward. If working the obliques is not desired, keep

the knee joints safe by pivoting the feet and knees in the same direction.

KEY WORDS

Muscle balance
Skeletal framework
Muscle groups

Opposing muscles
Muscle pairs

Safety
Contraindicated

SUMMARY

—Muscle imbalances reflect differences in the relative strengths and flexibilities of the various muscles surrounding a joint or body part.

—The human body is designed to be balanced in all ways.

—The most important factor in successful aquatic exercise programming is a basic understanding of why each movement is being used.

—Participants should remember to work opposing muscles of a pair at least equally.

—Safety is another reason for knowing why a move is used.

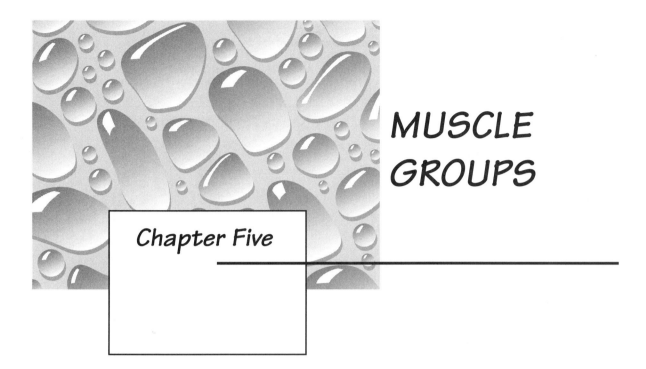

MUSCLE GROUPS

Chapter Five

ALIGNMENT AND MUSCLE BALANCE

Good postural **alignment** allows the human body to move safely. From a front view, the shoulders should evenly align over the hip joints, and the pelvis should rest over the hip joints in a balanced position. From the side, the spine should have an anterior curve in the cervical and lumbar areas and a posterior curve in the thoracic area. The ear, shoulder, hip, and ankle joints should fall in line. When deviation from good postural alignment exists in one area, there is always a reactive deviation in another area.

Aquatic exercisers should not only practice proper postural alignment, but the exercises used should promote **muscle balance.** Muscles should be strong enough to contract fully when needed and to relax fully when contraction is not needed. Muscles that are **hypertoned** are unable to relax fully.

All the muscles surrounding each joint should be toned equally so there is good balance and give and take among them. Each muscle should be of appropriate resting length, so that bones and other body parts hang in proper neutral positions.

Muscles that are subjected to repeated overload adapt by becoming stronger and wider. Unless they are specifically overloaded with a stretch, they also become permanently tighter and shorter. When one muscle is consistently strengthened and the opposing muscle ignored, the strengthened muscle becomes permanently shortened and the opposing or antagonistic muscle remains lengthened, weak, and inefficient.

Muscle groups at a joint often work in pairs to first flex and then extend a part of the body. A good example of a **flexor/extensor pair** is the hamstring/quadricep muscle group. The hamstrings flex (bend) the knee, and the quadriceps straighten (extend) it.

Muscle balance is achieved when both muscles in a pair are developed to the same degree. Imbalance, resulting from overdevelopment or underdevelopment of one member of the pair, can cause poor posture, pain, tendon tightness, and eventual misalignment of the body's framework.

MOVEMENTS FOR MAJOR MUSCLE GROUPS

The rest of this chapter outlines the major muscle groups. Each section ends with a list of toning, aerobic, arm, and stretch movements. (See descriptions of most in Chapter 4.)

When designing a workout, be sure to include at least two moves for each major muscle group in every hour-long program.

1. *Pectoralis / Trapezius / Rhomboids*
The **pectorals** are the chest muscles. The **trapezius** is a diamond-shaped muscle in the upper back and neck. The **rhomboids** are small-back muscles located beneath the trapezius.

The exercises listed below work the trapezius, rhomboids, and pectorals. When arm movements go in front of or across the front of the body, they work the pectorals. When they move toward the sides and back, they work the trapezius and rhomboids.

DIAGRAM 5–1 Pectorals

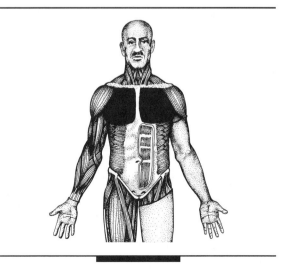

DIAGRAM 5–2 Trapexius

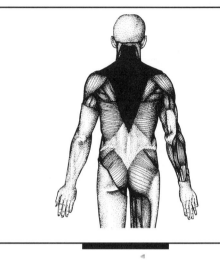

—elbow press single
—elbow press with forearm down
—safe arms
—over and present
—scissor arms
—backstroke
—wind-up and present
—bow and arrow
—reach pull in
—stroke
—waterpull
—shoulder shrug
—backstroke side

2. *Hamstrings / Quadriceps*
The **hamstrings** are located in the back of each thigh. The **quadriceps** are located in the front of each thigh.

The exercises listed below work the quadriceps and hamstrings: the hamstrings, as the knee is bent, and the quadriceps, as the knee is straightened.

—jazzkick
—flick kick
—jig
—hoedown
—hopscotch

DIAGRAM 5–3   Quadriceps/Hamstrings

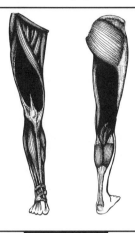

- heel hits behind
- heel hits across
- mule kick
- ski bounce
- paddlekick
- forward lunge
- Russian kick

3. *Biceps/Triceps*

The **biceps** are located on the front of each upper arm. The **triceps** are located on the back of each upper arm.

DIAGRAM 5–4   Biceps/Triceps

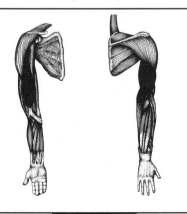

The exercises listed below will work the biceps and triceps. As the elbow bends, the biceps will contract. As the elbow straightens, the triceps contract.

- waist curl
- tricep extensions back (also forward, out)
- side press out, in
- jog arms
- lateral push
- backstroke

4. *Iliopsoas/Gluteals*

The **iliopsoas** (hip flexors) are located on the front of the hip. The **gluteus maximus** (called the **gluteals**) are located on the buttocks.

The exercises listed below work the iliopsoas when the hip flexes or the leg moves forward. As the leg comes back and lowers through the water, the gluteals contract.

- tuck jump
- frog jump
- kick
- kick corner
- kneelift
- back kick (swing)

DIAGRAM 5–5   Iliopsoas/Gluteus Maximus

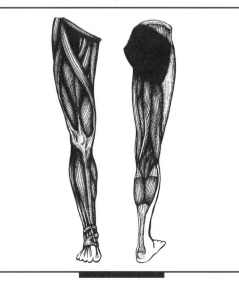

—scissors
—knee swing
—back lunge
—leap forward
—forward train
—forward walking/jogging movements
—flutter kick
—scissor jump

5. *Adductors/Abductors*
    The **adductors** are located on each inner thigh. The **abductors** are located on the outside of each thigh.
    The exercises listed below work the hip adductors and abductors. As the limb moves laterally, the abductors contract. As the limb returns to anatomical position, the adductors contract.

—crossing jog
—side kick
—side circles
—jumping jacks
—cross kick
—heel hits front
—fling
—fling kick
—knee swing crossing

—wringer
—leap side
—rock side
—side train
—side step

6. *Obliques*
    The **obliques** are located under and to the side of the rectus abdominus muscle. They are midriff muscles.
    The exercises listed below work the obliques.

—waterpull
—twist
—karate punch
—press down and behind with sidebend
—over and present
—side scissors
—rock side
—leap side
—scissor turn
—swing twist
—ski bounce

DIAGRAM 5–7   Obliques

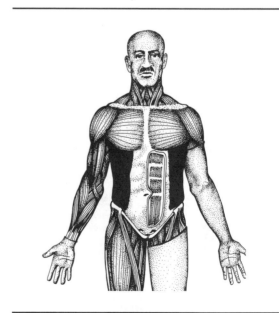

DIAGRAM 5–6   Adductors/Abductors

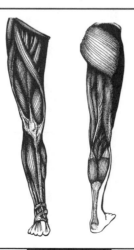

DIAGRAM 5–8   Rectus Abdominus

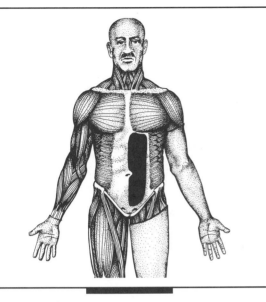

DIAGRAM 5–9   Deltoids

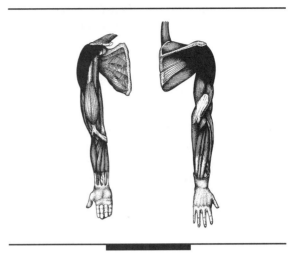

7.   *Abdominals / Erector Spinae*

The **erector spinae** is a large back muscle. The **abdominals** *(rectus abdominus)* is a large muscle located from the ribs to the pelvis.

There is a misconception that exercises that flex the hip are abdominal exercises. The rectus abdominus does not cross the hip joint and therefore is not the primary mover in hip flexion.

The exercises listed below will work the abdominals and back muscles.

- knees tucked crunch
- lift hips
- heel jack
- heel tilt
- pelvic tilt
- curl down
- jog tilt

8.   *Deltoids (Medial) / Latissimus Dorsi*

The **medial deltoid** is a cap on the shoulder. The **latissimus dorsi** is a large back muscle in the middle on each side of the back.

The exercises listed below will work the medial deltoid and latissimus dorsi. As the arms lift (abduct), the deltoid contracts. As they lower (adduct), the latissimus dorsi contracts.

- press down behind
- press down front
- press down alternate
- press down (one front, one back)
- press down with elbows bent

DIAGRAM 5–10   Latissimus Dorsi

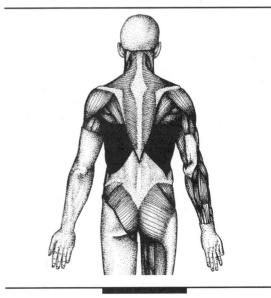

9. *Anterior and Posterior Deltoids*

The **anterior deltoids** are located on the front of each shoulder. The **posterior deltoids** are located on the back of each shoulder.

The exercises listed below will work the anterior deltoids as the arm moves forward and the posterior deltoids as the arm moves backward.

— armswing, forward and backward
— with both elbows bent or straight arms
— swing forward and backward, alternating arms forward and backward

10. *Gastrocnemius / Tibialis Anterior*

The **gastrocnemius** is located in the calf of each lower leg. The **tibialis anterior** is located in the front of each lower leg.

The exercises listed below will work the gastrocnemius as the toe points down (plantarflexes) and the tibialis anterior as the toe points up toward the shin (dorsiflexes).

— bounce
— most jogs
— heel jack

DIAGRAM 10–11 Gastrocneumius

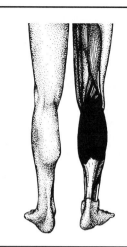

— heel tilt
— scissor with front toe up
— swing twist with toe up
— kick and point, kick and flex

KEY WORDS

Alignment	Quadriceps	Abdominals
Muscle balance	Biceps	Erector spinae
Hypertoned	Triceps	Medial deltoids
Flexor/extensor pair	Iliopsoas	Latissimus dorsi
Pectorals	Gluteals	Anterior deltoids
Trapezius	Adductors	Posterior deltoids
Rhomboids	Abductors	Gastrocnemius
Hamstrings	Obliques	Tibialis anterior

SUMMARY

— Good postural alignment allows the human body to move safely.
— Aquatic exercisers should not only practice proper postural alignment, but the exercises they use should promote muscle balance.

— Each muscle should be of appropriate resting length, so that the bones and other body parts hang in proper neutral positions.
— Muscle groups often work in pairs to first flex and then extend a part of the body at a joint.

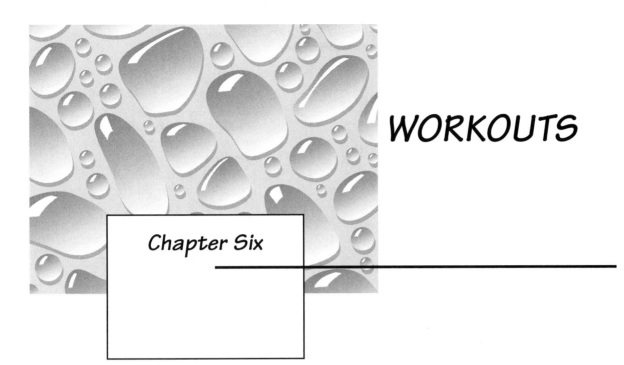

WORKOUTS

Chapter Six

SAMPLE CLASS PROGRAMS

Strength Training

— Thermal Warm-Up

Do the following for 1 minute each:
A. Jog or walk, forward and back (usually, 8 or 16 jogs forward and 8 or 16 jogs backward, depending on pool size)
B. Continue jogging or walking, bending the knee and pulling the heel back to the buttock
C. Continue jogging or walking, using high kneelifts
D. Change to walking or jogging sideways (8 or 16 to the right, 8 or 16 to the left)
E. Jumping jacks with arms beneath the water surface

— Prestretch

Hold the following stretches for 10 to 15 seconds each:
A. Quadricep right, quadricep left
B. Hamstring right, hamstring left
C. Calf right, calf left
D. Hip flexor right, hip flexor left
E. Pectorals
F. Trapezius

— Weight Training

1. Do the following for 90 seconds each with force:
   A. Bicep curls up
   B. Tricep extensions down
   C. Pectoral presses (elbow press forward) with elbows bent
   D. Trapezius/rhomboid pulls (elbow press back) with elbows bent
   E. Latissimus dorsi presses (press down behind)
   F. Deltoid lifts

2. Do the following with the right leg for 90 seconds each with force; then repeat with the left leg:
   A. Knee flexion (mule kick)
   B. Hip flexion (kick forward)

C. Hip abduction (side lift)
D. Knee extension (flick kick)
E. Hip extension (back kick)
F. Hip adduction (cross kick)
G. Hip circumduction (circles)

— Cooldown

Walk for 2 to 3 minutes.

— Poststretch

Do the following stretches for 20 to 30 seconds each:

A. Quadricep stretch, right and left
B. Gluteal stretch, right and left
C. Abductor stretch, right and left
D. Hamstring stretch, right and left
E. Iliopsoas stretch, right and left
F. Adductor stretch, right and left
G. Bicep stretch
H. Tricep stretch, right and left
I. Pectoral stretch
J. Trapezius stretch
K. Deltoid (medial) stretch, right and left

Water Walking

Wearing shoes is recommended.

— Thermal Warm-Up

Do the following for 45 seconds each:

A. Walk with small steps, 12 forward and 12 backward, using walking arms (the right arm swings forward as the left leg steps forward), elbows bent.
B. Repeat A with shoulder rolls.
C. Walk forward in a circle, rolling from heel to toe
D. Walk backward in a circle, rolling from toe to heel.
E. Walk forward around the circle on the toes.
F. Walk backward around the circle on the heels.
G. Do toe circles for 20 seconds with the right foot and 20 seconds with the left foot.

— Prestretch

A. Calf stretch, right and left (15 seconds each)
B. Walk forward around the circle; push both arms forward for trapezius/rhomboid stretch (20 seconds)
C. Walk backward around the circle, using a shoulder blade pinch to stretch the pectorals (20 seconds)
D. Walk forward to the right corner; walk back using mule kicks (20 seconds)
E. Repeat D to the left corner and back (20 seconds)
F. Quadricep stretch, right and left (15 seconds each)
G. Hip flexor stretch, right and left (15 seconds each)
H. Hamstring stretch, right and left (15 seconds each)
I. Calf stretch, right and left (15 seconds each)
J. Walk forward and backward using sidebends (30 seconds)

— Cardiovascular Warm-Up

1. Do the following in circle formation for 45 seconds each:
    A. Moving forward, take exaggerated, long strides, keeping the knees bent. Add jogging arms, with the hands cupped.
    B. Keep the knees bent and move double time with smaller steps. Change the arms to punching.
    C. Repeat A and B.
2. Face the center of the circle, and do the following for 45 seconds each:
    A. Walk sideways using lateral push arms. Move 8 to the right and 8 to the left repeatedly until the time allotment is finished.
    B. Walk sideways using deltoid lift arms. Move 8 to the right and 8 to the left repeatedly until the time allotment is finished.
    C. Walk in and out of the circle using breaststroke and backstroke arms.

D. Add high knees to 2C and continue.

E. Straighten the legs to a goose step, moving in and out of the circle.

F. Repeat B, C, D, and E.

— Aerobics

Do the following exercises for 60 seconds each:

Group 1—In scatter formation:

A. Walk forward on the toes (bent elbow, walking arms); walk back on the heels.

B. Walk sideways using sidekicks. Move 8 to the right and 8 to the left repeatedly until the time allotment is finished.

C. Walk forward and back using mule kicks.

Group 2—In scatter formation:

A. Walk in a square with the knees and toes pointed somewhat out.

B. Repeat A, moving backward.

C. Walk forward and backward, using side bends.

D. Walk, leaning forward while moving forward and leaning backward while moving backward.

Group 3—In circle formation:

A. Walk forward into the circle, using high knees.

B. Continue with high knees, but cross the right foot over the left and lower the right as the step is taken (strut).

C. Walk backward around the circle, crossing the right foot behind the left and the left behind the right.

Group 4—In circle formation:

A. Walk around the circle, using high knees.

B. Continue walking around the circle, but change to a goose step.

C. Continue walking around the circle, but change to a flick kick.

D. Repeat A through C, moving backward around the circle.

Group 5—In circle formation:

A. Walk around the circle, contracting and releasing the abdominals.

B. Walk backward, using diagonal kicks.

C. Move forward, using sidekicks and stepping across.

D. Turn around and go back (again, facing forward), using sidekicks and stepping behind.

— Cooldown

Do the following in scatter formation for 1 minute each:

A. Walk 4 low and 4 high (2 sets forward and 2 sets back).

B. Walk 4 fast and 8 slow, forward and back.

C. Walk sideways, 2 slow and 4 fast (2 sets right, 2 sets left).

D. Over and present.

E. Walk forward and back, using shoulder rolls.

— Upper-Body Toning

Do the following for 45 seconds each (3-1/2 minutes total):

A. Elbow press

B. Elbow press back

C. Bicep curls

D. Tricep extensions

E. Push across

— Edge-of-Pool Toning

Do the following for 1 minute each:

A. Side lifts—Do 10 with force on the lift out and 10 with force on the return. Repeat.

B. Knee flexion (mule kick)—Do 10 with force on pulling the heel back and 10 with force on straightening the leg.

C. Knee swings

D. Turn the other side to the pool edge and repeat with the other leg.

— Stretch

Hold each for 30 seconds (5 minutes total):
A. Quadricep stretch, right and left
B. Calf stretch, right and left
C. Hamstring stretch, right and left
D. Pectoral stretch
E. Iliopsoas stretch, right and left
F. Back stretch, push forward
G. Adductor stretch, right and left

Aerobics

Do the following workout 3 times on nonconsecutive days:

— Thermal Warm-Up

Do the following for 1 minute each (4 minutes total):
A. Hoedowns
B. Jazz kicks
C. Sidekicks
D. Cross kicks

— Stretch

Do the following for 15 seconds each (3 minutes total):
A. Quadricep stretch, right and left
B. Calf stretch, right and left
C. Hamstring stretch, right and left
D. Pectoral stretch
E. Iliopsoas stretch, right and left
F. Back stretch
G. Adductor stretch, right and left

— Cardiovascular Warm-Up

Do the following for five minutes total:
A. Hopscotches, 1 minute
B. Sidekicks (repeat 4 left, 4 right), 1 minute
C. Forward kicks, slow and fast, 2 minutes
D. Kneelifts fast, 1 minute

— Aerobics

Do each of the following for 60 seconds:

Group 1
— Jumping jacks
— Jumping jacks crossing
— Forward kicks fast
— Forward kicks slow

Group 2
— Sidekicks
— Mule kicks fast
— Mule kicks doubles
— Flick kicks (repeat 8 left, 8 right)
— Jazzkicks

Group 3
— Diagonal kicks fast
— Diagonal kicks slow
— Diagonal kicks slow (repeat 4 left, 4 right)
— Jog forward slow and backward fast
— Jumping jacks, slow and fast

Group 4
— Scissors
— Scissors with front toes up
— Scissors with back toes down
— Jog tilt (8 leaning forward, 8 leaning backward)
— Kneelifts

— Cooldown

Do the following for 1 minute each (3 minutes total):
A. Jog in place, fast and slow
B. Rock from side to side
C. Mule kicks

— Upper-Body Toning

Do the following for 45 seconds each (3-1/2 minutes total):

A. Elbow press
B. Elbow press back
C. Bicep curls
D. Tricep extensions
E. Push across

— Edge-of-Pool Toning

Do the following for 1 minute each:

A. Side lifts—Do 10 with force on the lift out and 10 with force on the return in. Repeat.
B. Knee flexion (mule kick)—Do 10 with force on pulling the heel back and 10 with force on straightening the leg.
C. Knee swings
D. Turn the other side to the pool edge and repeat with the other leg.

— Stretch

Hold each for 30 seconds (5 minutes total):
A. Quadricep stretch, right and left
B. Calf stretch, right and left
C. Hamstring stretch, right and left
D. Pectoral stretch
E. Iliopsoas stretch, right and left
F. Back stretch, push forward
G. Adductor stretch, right and left

Toning

— Thermal Warm-Up

A. Walk fast in a big circle, moving clockwise, for 30 seconds.
B. Move back around the circle for 30 seconds.
C. Walk fast with high knees, moving counterclockwise, for 30 seconds.
D. Back up for 30 seconds.
E. Walk sideways, moving right 8 to 10 steps and then left 8 to 10 steps, for 1 minute
F. Walk with sidebends around the circle for 30 seconds.
G. Back up with sidebends for 30 seconds.
H. Walk around the circle counterclockwise, kicking the heel toward the buttocks, for 30 seconds.
I. Back up, kicking the heel toward the buttocks, for 30 seconds.
J. Walk around the circle on the heels for 30 seconds.
K. Back up around the circle on the heels for 30 seconds.

— Prestretch

Hold each of the following for 15 to 20 seconds:
A. Calf stretch, right and left
B. Iliopsoas stretch, right and left
C. Hamstring stretch, right and left
D. Quadricep stretch, right and left
E. Adductor stretch, right and left
F. Pectoral stretch
G. Back stretch

— Toning

At the pool edge, do each of the following for 24 reps or 1 minute. Do those exercises that are repeated on the right and left sides for 1 minute on each side.
A. Bicep curls, right and left
B. Mule kicks, right and left
C. Tricep extensions, right and left
D. Flick kicks, right and left
E. Swing the arms, forward and backward (with emphasis on arm extension or pull back)
F. Kickswing, right and left (with emphasis on hip extension)
G. Deltoid lift (both arms together)
H. Side lifts, right and left (hip abduction)
I. Press down (both arms together)
J. Cross kicks, right and left
K. Elbow press forward
L. Abdominal crunches
M. Elbow press back
N. Kick swing, right and left (with emphasis on hip flexion or kick)
O. Swing the arms together, forward and backward (with emphasis on swing forward or shoulder flexion)
P. Punch across (alternating arms)

— Cooldown and Poststretch

A. Do A and B from Warm-Up
B. Bicep stretch, 15 to 20 seconds
C. Trapezius stretch, 15 to 20 seconds
D. Do C and D from Warm-Up

E. Quadricep stretch, right and left
F. Hip flexor stretch, right and left
G. Do E from Warm-Up with tricep stretch, right and left, and neck stretch, right and left
H. Do F and G from Warm-Up
 I. Abductor stretch, right and left
J. Adductor stretch, right and left
K. Do H and I from Warm-Up
L. Hamstring stretch, right and left
M. Calf stretch, right and left
N. Back stretch

Flexibility

— Warm-Up

Do the following in circle formation:
A. Walk fast, moving clockwise, for 30 seconds.
B. Back up for 30 seconds.
C. Walk fast with high knees, moving counterclockwise, for 30 seconds.
D. Back up for 30 seconds.
E. Walk sideways, moving 8 to 10 steps to the right and 8 to 10 steps to the left, for 1 minute.
F. Walk forward with sidebends around the circle for 30 seconds.
G. Back up with sidebends.
H. Walk, kicking the heels toward the buttocks, moving counterclockwise, for 30 seconds.
 I. Back up, kicking the heels toward the buttocks, for 30 seconds.

— Arms

Use the following arm movements with A through I above:
A. Tricep extensions
B. Bicep curls
C. Punching the opposite arm forward
D. Backstrokes
E. Deltoid lifts
F & G. Press downs
H & I. Swing the corresponding arm forward and up and the opposite arm down and backward.

— Flexibility

Upper Body—Jog or walk while doing the following stretches to keep body temperature at a comfortable level. If the body becomes chilled and muscles tighten, stop stretching and go through the Warm-Up phase more vigorously until body temperature is warm enough for comfortable, relaxed stretching.

Hold each of the following for 20 to 30 seconds:

A. Push both arms up, lifting from the ribs
B. Trapezius stretch
C. Pectoral stretch
D. Tricep stretch, right and left
E. Bicep stretch
F. Neck stretch, right and left
G. Walk with shoulder rolls

Lower Body—Hold each of the following stretches for 30 seconds:

A. Do C and D from the Warm-Up
B. Iliopsoas stretch, right and left
C. Gluteal stretch, right and left
D. Do E from the Warm-Up
E. Adductor stretch, right and left
F. Abductor stretch, right and left
G. Do F and G from the Warm-Up
H. Oblique stretch, right and left
 I. Do H and I from the Warm-Up
J. Quadricep stretch, right and left
K. Hamstring stretch, right and left
L. Walk forward on the toes and backward on the heels for 1 minute
M. Calf stretch, right and left
N. Tibialis anterior stretch, right and left
O. Back stretch
P. Abdominal stretch

— Cooldown

Walk slowly around the pool for 3 minutes.

Aqua Circuit Training

— Thermal Warm-Up

Do each of the following for 1 minute:
A. Jumping jacks and sidekicks
B. Kneelifts moving forward, crosskicks back
C. Heelhits, front and back
D. Kneeswing combo in place, up and back (4 right, 4 left), cross (4 right, 4 left)

— Prestretch

Do each of the following for 10 to 15 seconds:
A. Quadricep stretch, right and left
B. Iliopsoas stretch, right and left
C. Hamstring stretch, right and left
D. Scissors with pectoral stretch
E. Calf stretch, right and left
F. Back stretch

— Cardiovascular Warm-Up

Do each of the following for 1 minute:
A. Kicks, slow and fast
B. Jumping jacks crossing
C. Slides (16 right, 16 left)
D. Ski bounces
E. Swing twists in 3

— Aerobics

For each of the following, spend 1 minute doing each station movement and 2 minutes doing each aerobic segment:

- *First station*—Elbow press, forward and backward
- *Aerobics*—Jog forward, heelhits back (any mix); add jazzkick
- *Second station*—Mule kicks, right leg
- *Aerobics*—Swing twist singles and doubles (any mix); vary with the toes of the back foot down and the toes of the front foot up; move forward and backward and side to side
- *Third station*—Bicep curls, tricep extensions
- *Aerobics*—Side steps and scissors (any mix)
- *Fourth station*—Mule kicks, left leg
- *Aerobics*—Bounce square; add scissors moving forward, jumping jacks back
- *Fifth station*—Kickswings, right leg
- *Aerobics*—Sidekicks, 4 right and 4 left
- *Sixth station*—Deltoid lifts, press down
- *Aerobics*—Jump bounce, 4 forward and 4 back; add kicks, slow and fast
- *Seventh station*—Kickswings, left leg
- *Aerobics*—Slide; add kicks forward, ski bounces back
- *Eighth station*—Side leglifts, right leg
- *Aerobics*—Mule kicks, slow and fast; add jumping jacks and jumping jacks crossing
- *Ninth station*—Side leglifts, left leg
- *Aerobics*—Back kicks, slow and fast; add back kicks forward, kneelifts back
- *Tenth station*—Abdominal crunches
- *Aerobics*—Kicks and fling kicks; add flings and heelhits front
- *Eleventh station*—Crosskicks, right leg
- *Aerobics*—Rockinghorse 7 and up; add tuck jumps
- *Twelfth station*—Crosskicks, left leg
- *Aerobics*—Kneelifts forward, heel hits back, slow and fast; add rocking side to side
- *Thirteenth station*—Flick kicks, right leg
- *Aerobics*—Jumping jacks square, 4 each direction (right, back, left, forward); add crossing kneelifts, 4 right and 4 left
- *Fourteenth station*—Flick kicks, left leg
- *Aerobics*—Scissors and ski bounces

— Cooldown and Flexibility

Do the following and hold the stretches for 20 to 30 seconds each:

A. Swing twists with flag arms
B. Walk 8 forward, kick, walk 8 backward; repeat 3 times
C. Bounce 8 times
D. Adductor stretch, right and left
E. Side step with tricep stretch
F. Side step with neck stretch
G. Side step with shoulder stretch

H. Swing twist 16 times
I. Iliopsoas stretch, right and left
J. Kneeswing combo, 4 sets
K. Hamstring stretch, right and left
L. Pectoral stretch
M. Corner jazzkick 32 times
N. Quadricep stretch, right and left
O. Back stretch
P. Heel jacks 32 times
Q. Calf stretch, right and left
R. Push both arms up

Sport Specific

— Thermal Warm-Up

Do each of the following for 1 minute:
A. Walk with long, exertive strides, forward and backward.
B. Jog forward and back, with high knees. Use bicep curls and tricep extensions.
C. Sidestep 8 to 10 steps to the right and 8 to 10 steps to the left. Use deltoid lift and press down arms.
D. Jog in place, with heels kicking up and back (like mule kicks). Use elbow press forward and backward.

— Prestretch

Hold each of the following for 10 to 15 seconds:
A. Calf stretch, right and left
B. Iliopsoas stretch, right and left
C. Hamstring stretch, right and left
D. Back stretch

— Cardiovascular Warm-Up

Do the following combination movements/stretches:
A. Do 16 sidesteps to the right while doing a tricep stretch right.
B. Do 16 sidesteps to the left while doing a tricep stretch left.
C. Repeat A and B.
D. Do 32 jumping jacks while doing a pectoral stretch.
E. Do 32 jumping jacks while doing a deltoid lift and press down.
F. Do 8 jumping jacks moving forward and 8 moving back; repeat this sequence (8 up, 8 back) 4 times.
G. Do 32 scissors.

— Aerobics

Balance and Coordination
A. Do 32 ski bounces while doing tricep extensions.
B. Do 16 ski bounces moving forward and 16 moving backward; repeat this sequence (16 up, 16 back) 4 times.
C. Do 32 ski bounces in place with the right foot only.
D. Repeat C with the left leg.
E. Bounce 4 times moving sideways to the right and 4 times moving sideways to the left; add the lateral press arm movement. Repeat this sequence (4 right, 4 left) 4 times.
F. Repeat E using only the right foot.
G. Repeat E using only the left foot.
H. Bounce 16 times in a square, so that the first bounce makes the right corner of the square (bounce right, back, left, forward to make the square). Bounce another 16, so that the first bounce makes the left corner of the square (bounce left, back, right, forward). Add the jump rope arm movement.
I. Repeat H using the right leg only.
J. Repeat H using the left leg only.

Intervals
A. Do scissors at moderate intensity for 30 seconds; swing the arms alternately forward and backward.
B. Do scissors at high intensity for 30 seconds. Use more power, lengthen the stride, use a larger range of motion with the arms, and push up off the pool bottom with more effort.
C. Repeat A and B (3 times).

Power

A. Do tuck jumps, 8 moving forward and 8 moving backward. Do the sequence (8 up, 8 back) covering a moderate amount of distance and twice covering the largest distance possible.

B. Do jump bounces, 1 forward and 1 backward; do 16 sets.

C. Do 3 small bounces and 1 big jump, covering a maximum distance on the big jump. Move 4 forward and 4 backward; repeat this sequence (4 up, 4 back) 4 times.

D. Run with long strides to form a circle; move forward around the circle for 2 minutes.

Intervals

A. Do jumping jacks at moderate intensity for 30 seconds.

B. Do jumping jacks at high intensity for 30 seconds.

C. Repeat A and B (3 more times).

Sport Stations

Spend 1 minute each at 4 different stations of your choice:

A. Baseball bats

B. Tennis racquets

C. Power mule kick drills

D. Basketball jumps

E. Run and hurdle

F. Sprinting

G. Run and long jump

H. Golf clubs

— Cooldown and Flexibility

A. Walk for 2 minutes with varied strides.

B. Sidestep 16 to the right while doing a right shoulder stretch.

C. Sidestep 16 to the left while doing a left shoulder stretch.

D. Sidestep 16 to the right while doing a right tricep stretch.

E. Sidestep 16 to the left while doing a left tricep stretch.

F. Calf stretch, right and left, 15 seconds each

G. Do 24 scissors.

H. Iliopsoas stretch, right and left, 15 seconds each

I. Hamstring stretch, right and left, 15 seconds each

J. Do 24 jumping jacks.

K. Back stretch, 15 seconds

L. Pectoral stretch, 15 seconds

M. Repeat A.

Bench Aerobics

— Thermal Warm-Up

Do each of the following for 1 minute:

A. Walk forward and backward, using tricep extensions and bicep curls.

B. Sidestep 8 right and 8 left, using deltoid lift and lateral press.

C. Jog forward 16 using mule kicks; jog backward 16 with kneelifts.

D. Jumping jacks

— Prestretch

Hold each of the following 10 to 15 seconds:

A. Calf stretch, right and left

B. Quadricep stretch, right and left

C. Iliopsoas stretch, right and left

D. Hamstring stretch, right and left

E. Pectoral stretch

F. Back stretch

— Cardiovascular Warm-Up

Do each of the following:

A. Jog out and in, 8 sets

B. Kneelifts, 32 reps

C. Sidekicks, 32 reps

D. Back kicks, 32 reps

E. Kneeswings (8 right, 8 left), 4 sets

F. Jog out and in, 8 sets

– Aerobics

Do each of the following for 1 minute:

A. Step up, up, down, down, leading with the right foot.
B. Do jumping jacks without the bench.
C. Step up, up, down, down, leading with the left foot.
D. Do jumping jacks without the bench.
E. Step up, hold, down, down, alternating the right and left feet on the "up" step (right foot steps up, left foot steps down, right foot steps down, left foot steps up, right foot steps down, left foot steps down). Hold the "up" for 2 counts.
F. Do kneelifts without the bench.
G. With the right side to the bench, step up and down, with the right foot always stepping up on the bench and the left foot always stepping down on the pool bottom.
H. Do scissors without the bench.
I. With the left side to the bench, step up and down, with the left foot always stepping up on the bench and the right foot always stepping down on the pool bottom.
J. Do scissors without the bench.
K. With legs straddling the bench, do jumping jacks. (This move should not be done if the bench is in waist-deep water.)
L. Walk around the bench in a circle, moving clockwise. (Do not step up or down on the bench.)
M. With legs straddling the bench, step down, up, up, hold, alternating the right and left feet on the "down" step (right foot steps down, left foot steps up, right foot steps up, left foot steps down, right foot steps up, left foot steps up). Hold the second "up" for 2 counts.
N. Do sidekicks without the bench.
O. Step up, kneelift, step down, step down, alternating the right and left feet on the step "up" (step up with the right foot, kneelift with the left leg, step down with the left foot, step down with the right foot; repeat this sequence with the opposite foot).
P. Do back kicks without the bench.
Q. With legs straddling the bench, step up, kick, step down, step down, alternating the on the step "up" (step up with the right foot, kick forward with the left leg, step down with the left foot, step down with the right foot; repeat this sequence with the opposite foot).
R. Do jumping jacks without the bench.

– Cooldown

Do each of the following for 1 minute:

A. Walk forward and backward, using tricep extensions and bicep curls.
B. Walk forward and backward with high kneelifts.
C. Sidestep, right and left
D. Sidekicks
E. Kneeswing 8 right and 8 left until the time allotment is up.

– Flexibility

Hold each of the following for 10 to 15 seconds:

A. Calf stretch, right and left
B. Iliopsoas stretch, right and left
C. Quadricep stretch, right and left
D. Hamstring stretch, right and left
E. Abductor stretch, right and left
F. Pectoral stretch
G. Back stretch

Deep Water: Using Flotation Vests or Belts

– Thermal Warm-Up

Do each of the following for 1 minute:

A. Jog forward at moderate intensity, using tricep extensions.
B. Jog backward at moderate intensity, using bicep curls.

C. Do jumping jacks with deltoid lifts and press downs.

D. Do scissors, with arms alternately swinging forward and backward.

— Prestretch

Do each of the following for 10 to 15 seconds:
A. Hamstring stretch, right and left
B. Quadricep stretch, right and left
C. Iliopsoas stretch, right and left
D. Pectoral stretch
E. Back stretch
F. Calf stretch, right and left (at the edge of the pool, pressing the foot of the leg to be stretched against the pool wall)

— Cardiovascular Warm-Up

Do each of the following for 1 minute:
A. Jog with high knees, staying in place.
B. Jog with high knees, moving forward by using breaststroke arms.
C Jog with high knees, moving backward by using backstroke arms.
D. Jog with heels kicking up and back (mule kick), staying in place.
E. Repeat D, moving forward using breaststroke arms. (The abdominals must be contracted, and no hip flexion should occur.)
F. Repeat D, moving backward using backstroke arms.

— Aerobics

1. Do each of the following for 1 minute:
   A. Scissors at moderate intensity, staying in place
   B. Scissors, moving forward by using crawl arms
   C. Scissor jumps, using enough force to push the body up and out of the water
   D. Scissors, moving backward by using single arms alternating the backstroke

2. Do each of the following:
   A. Scissor and jumping jack combo (1 scissor, 1 jumping jack); repeat for 1 minute
   B. Kneelifts in 3, 4 sets in place and 4 sets moving forward; 4 sets in place and 4 sets moving backward
   C. Scissors, 16 times each: toes pointed out, toes pointed down, toes pointed up. Repeat this sequence (16 out, 16 down, 16 up) 2 times
   D. Mule kicks, 16 moving forward, kneelifts, 16 moving backward; repeat this sequence (16 forward, kneelifts, 16 backward) 4 times
   E. Scissors, 16 with long, slow strides, 16 with short, fast strides; repeat this sequence (16 long, 16 short) 2 times

3. Do each of the following for 1 minute:
   A. Jumping jacks in place
   B. Jumping jacks, moving forward using breaststroke arms (the abdominals must be contracted, and hip hyperextension should not occur)
   C. Jumping jacks (legs should close with enough force to push the body up and out of the water)
   D. Jumping jacks, moving backward using backstroke arms
   E. Jumping jacks crossing
   F. Jumping jacks, alternating with toes pointed down and up

— Cooldown

Do each of the following for 1 minute:
A. Jog forward with mule kicks
B. Jog backward with kneelifts
C. Mule kicks in place
D. Kneelifts in place
E. Heel hits in front
F. Heel hits behind

— Toning and Flexibility

1. Work at the edge of the pool, with one side to the pool wall (work the same side, right or left, for entire sequence). Repeat each movement 32 times; hold each stretch for 15 seconds.
   A. Side leglift
   B. Adductor stretch
   C. Kickswing
   D. Iliopsoas stretch
   E. Side leg circles
   F. Abductor stretch
   G. Mule kicks
   H. Hamstring stretch

2. Switch sides, turning the other side to the pool wall. Repeat A through H. Again, repeat each movement 32 times; hold each stretch for 15 seconds.

3. Continue as follows:
   A. With the back to the pool edge, do elbow presses forward and backward
   B. With the back still to the pool edge, do pectoral stretch
   C. Facing the pool edge, do deltoid lifts and press downs
   D. Back stretch
   E. Calf stretch, right and left (press the foot of the leg being stretched against the pool wall)

WORKOUT INTENSITY

Chapter Seven

USING HEARTRATE TO MEASURE INTENSITY

The relationship between **heartrate** and workout intensity always has been an enigma. Program guidelines advise checking exertion levels during class. However, checking heartrates often seems counterproductive. Many students—especially fit ones—are disappointed to learn that their heartrates usually remain lower than the target range recommended for aerobic improvement. Checking perceived exertion does not seem to work either, because students often do not feel that they work as hard in a water exercise class as they do outside running or in a land-based aerobics class.

What is a participant to do? Exertion levels need to be checked, but doing so sometimes leads them to think that water workouts are wimpy. To solve this dilemma, students must have a thorough understanding of heartrates and their significance in aquatics classes.

Terms and Definitions

Several different terms are used to characterize heartrates:

- Resting heartrate (RHR)
- Maximal heartrate
- Working heartrate range
- Minimum working heartrate
- Maximum working heartrate
- Optimum working heartrate
- Target zone
- Recovery heartrate

Resting Heartrate

The **resting heartrate (RHR)** is the number of times the heart beats per minute when the body is at rest. This heartrate usually is counted over 60 seconds. The RHR should be measured before getting up in the morning or after sitting quietly for 20 minutes. To ensure an accurate RHR, the exercise participant should measure the resting heartrate on three separate occasions and take the average.

Maximal Heartrate

The **maximal heartrate** is the greatest number of times per minute the heart is capable of beating. It is the highest heartrate a person can attain during heavy exercise. An accurate measure of the maximal heartrate can be determined by a graded exercise test called a *stress electrocardiogram*. Exercise leaders who do not have access to, or the training necessary to do, a stress electrocardiogram often calculate maximal heartrate by subtracting the participant's age from 220. This number is the general estimation for the maximal heartrate.

Working Heartrate Range

The **working heartrate range** is the zone within which an individual needs to work for aerobic training to take place. It is the area between, and including, the minimum working heartrate and the maximum working heartrate. When the exercising heartrate remains in this zone, cardiorespiratory conditioning is likely to occur. The training intensity range often varies from as little as 50% to 85% of maximal oxygen consumption. A linear relationship exists between heartrate, oxygen consumption, and workload or workout intensity in most land-based exercise situations. Because of that, the *target zone* (target heartrate range or training zone) is used to determine when cardiorespiratory conditioning is occurring during exercise.

Several formulas currently are in use to determine the working heartrate range. The most common (discussed later) is the *Karvonen formula*.

The top of the target zone, which would be the upper limit of suggested exercise intensity, is the highest percentage. The low percentage is used to determine the minimum threshold to improve cardiorespiratory fitness. Students

who are unfit or just beginning exercise should use the low percentage or work at or above the minimum working heartrate. As conditioning occurs, students can work at a more comfortable intensity in the middle of the zone. Many internal and external factors affect a participant's heartrate. This zone is merely a guideline. Heartrate varies from person to person and situation to situation.

Minimum Working Heartrate

Minimum working heartrate is at the low end of the working heartrate range. This is the minimum number of times the heart should beat per minute during exercise for cardiorespiratory training to take place. It is sometimes referred to as the *threshold for aerobic training*. Students should know this number so they can work toward it during exercise.

Maximum Working Heartrate

The **maximum working heartrate** is at the upper end of the working heartrate range. This is the maximum number of times the heart should beat per minute during exercise for cardiorespiratory training to take place. Working at a higher level can be dangerous to individuals with known or unsuspected cardiorespiratory disease, and it does not promote efficient use of fats for fuel. Working at a rate higher than the maximum working heartrate is considered an anaerobic workout. The maximum working heartrate is often called the *anaerobic threshold*.

Optimum Working Heartrate

Optimum working heartrate is the ideal number of beats per minute for cardiorespiratory training to take place. There are different optimum working heartrates for different fitness goals. The optimum working heartrate always falls between the minimum working heartrate and the maximum working heartrate.

Target Zone

Target zone is another term for the working heartrate range.

Recovery Heartrate

The **recovery heartrate** is the number of times the heart beats per minute when monitored 5 to 10 minutes after vigorous exercise. It reflects how quickly the cardiorespiratory system returns to its preexercise condition. A more fit person recovers faster than a less fit person. The recovery heartrate often is used as an indicator of cardiorespiratory fitness.

Participants who do not recover to a normal range after five minutes have probably exercised too vigorously and are not conditioned enough to maintain that level for future exercise. They should be cautioned to exercise at a lower intensity during future exercise sessions.

Using Heartrates

It is important to understand heartrate terminology and formulas. Review the previous sections thoroughly to reinforce understanding of these concepts.

Scientists have found that the exercising heartrate often correlates closely to **oxygen consumption** (Pollack et al., 1982). Based on this correlation, a formula was developed for land-based exercise by a scientist named Karvonen that calculates the heartrate an individual must achieve in order to get desired benefits. The formula is adjusted for age and conditioning level. Aquatic exercisers also have begun to adapt it for their fitness programs.

Heartrates can be monitored easily by periodically taking the pulse during an exercise session and then adjusting the exercise intensity to bring the heartrate to the recommended level.

In order to use the formula, exercisers must be taught to monitor their heartrates. Begin by lightly pressing the index and middle fingers on the throat along the carotid artery.

Some exercisers prefer to place the fingers on the wrist at the radial pulse. At either site, the exerciser counts the pulsations while the instructor keeps track of time. While counting, the exerciser should be sure to continue to exercise by walking or jogging in place so that the heartrate does not slow down. The thumb should never be used to count pulsation, since it has a pulse of its own.

Formula for Determining Heartrate

Karvonen. The **Karvonen formula** is a scientific formula commonly accepted as the safest way to calculate the appropriate exertion level for land-based aerobic exercise. It is a relatively accurate and popular method of determining target heartrate. The Karvonen formula has an error rate of plus or minus 10 beats per minute when used on average individuals in land-based exercise. It is recommended by the American College of Sports Medicine (ACSM).

Actually measuring the maximal heartrate requires special equipment and trained personnel, whereas, the Karvonen formula uses

DIAGRAM 7–1 Karvonen Formula

$$\frac{\begin{array}{r} 220 \\ - \text{ age} \end{array}}{\textbf{Maximal heartrate}}$$

$$\frac{\begin{array}{r} \text{Maximal heartrate} \\ - \text{ Resting heartrate} \end{array}}{\textbf{Heartrate reserve}}$$

Heartrate reserve	Heartrate reserve
x .50 (Intensity level)	x .85 (Intensity level)
+ Resting heartrate	+ Resting heartrate
Minimum working heartrate	**Maximum working heartrate**

Target Zone

an age-predicted heartrate formula to arrive at the maximal heartrate. The formula is:

220 – age = Maximal heartrate

The age-predicted maximal heartrate formula estimates that 220 is the approximate maximal heartrate of a baby and that each year this rate decreases by one beat. For example, a 20-year-old person would have an estimated maximal heartrate of 200 beats per minute (220 – 20 = 200). A 40-year-old would have an estimated maximal heartrate of 180 (220 – 40 = 180). Although this is a commonly used formula, maximal heartrates often vary by plus or minus 10 beats per minute at any given age.

The Karvonen formula then goes on to calculate the heartrate reserve, which is the difference between the resting heartrate and the maximal heartrate. This portion of the formula is:

Maximal heartrate
— Resting heartrate
―――――――――――
Heartrate reserve

For example, a 40-year-old with a resting heartrate of 60 beats per minute would have a heartrate reserve of 120 (220 – 40 = 180; 180 – 60 = 120).

Once the heartrate reserve has been calculated for each participant, the Karvonen formula becomes simple. The target heartrate equals the heartrate reserve times the percentage of intensity plus the resting heartrate. The training intensity range used in the Karvonen formula is 50% to 85% of maximal heartrate reserve.

For example, a 40-year-old whose resting heartrate is 60 beats per minute is just beginning to exercise regularly and needs to know his or her minimum working heartrate. The heartrate reserve is multiplied by the intensity level, which in this case is 50%, to determine the minimum working heartrate plus the resting heartrate of 60 beats per minute (120 x .50 + 60 = 120). The minimum working heartrate for this exerciser is 120 beats per minute. The maximum working heartrate is determined in the same fashion, but 85% is used for intensity level (120 x .85 + 60 = 162). The maximum working heartrate for this exerciser is 162 beats per minute. The target zone for the exerciser is from 120 to 162 beats per minute.

Heartrate, Oxygen, and Caloric Consumption

Some students in aquatics classes feel they do not get as good a workout in water as they do on land. They definitely are wrong. They need education on heartrate, oxygen consumption, and caloric consumption.

Many students judge the intensity of a workout and, thus, the value of a class by the heartrate they achieve. If their heartrate is up, they are getting a good workout; if it isn't, they are not. Their mistake is assuming that heartrate is always an indication of workout intensity. This is not necessarily true. **Target heartrates are valid indicators of intensity only if they correlate with oxygen consumption.** Because we are aerobic beings, physiologists measure workout intensity, or energy expenditure, by measuring how much oxygen is utilized by the body during a given activity compared with how much oxygen is used at rest.

A given pace of exercise requires a specific amount of oxygen utilization. One quart of oxygen utilization equals 5 calories. If a participant wants to work at a 10-calorie-per-minute pace, he or she needs 2 quarts of oxygen per minute. The average outdoor walker uses 5 calories per minute, which would be 1 quart of oxygen per minute. The average outdoor jogger uses 10 calories per minute or 2 quarts per minute.

This information can make it simple for students to understand that **caloric consumption** is tied to oxygen consumption or utilization, not to heartrate. Heartrate is not always indicative of the amount of calories being burned. If caloric consumption is the exerciser's goal, he or she should increase his or her oxygen consumption, not necessarily his or her heartrate.

Unfortunately, oxygen consumption is measured with expensive, technical, cumbersome equipment that is attached to the exerciser with a breathing apparatus. It is impossible for exercisers outside a laboratory to check oxygen consumption.

That brings us back to heartrate. Heartrate is checked instead of oxygen consumption simply because everyone can do it easily. Formulas have been devised to correlate heartrate almost exactly to oxygen consumption if all conditions are ideal. Many land-based exercises, like running, biking, and aerobics, have almost ideal conditions and can use heartrate as their guide for workout intensity level.

Aquatic Heartrate

Students who participate in both land- and water-based exercise often find their heartrates lower from water exercise than land exercise, yet they receive the same benefits. There are no conclusive studies as to why this happens. There are, however, several commonly accepted theories under investigation.

Theories for Variations

1. **Heat dissipation**—When exercising, the body creates excess heat. The body gets rid of the heat through evaporation (sweat) and radiation (transferring heat to the skin, where it is radiated out to the environment). Because water dissipates heat more effectively than air, it is easier and, therefore, less stressful for the body to get rid of the excess heat in the water than on land. Moreover, less stress on the body results in a lower heartrate.

2. **Gravity**—Water lessens the effect of **gravity** on the body. Not only is it easier to spring up high in water, it

also is easier for the blood to be pumped uphill and back to the heart. This lessens the strain on the heart, resulting in a lower exercising heartrate.

3. **Compression**—Water acts like a compressor on the body, lending support. This extra compression is not limited to the superficial skin. It also penetrates to the deeper layers and organs of the body, including the blood vessels. This subtle compression on veins and arteries facilitates bloodflow while exercising, reducing stress on the heart and resulting in a lower working heartrate.

4. **Partial pressure**—Gases enter liquids more easily under pressure. Thus, oxygen is absorbed more easily into the blood during exercise. More efficient oxygen transfer may reduce the workload of the heart.

5. **Dive reflex**—A primitive reflex associated with a nerve found in the nasal area is called the dive reflex. When the face is submerged, this reflex lowers heartrate and blood pressure. This reflex is stronger in some individuals than others. Some research suggests that the face does not need to be in the water for the dive reflex to occur.

To compensate for the observed reduction in heartrate during water-based exercise, a variety of techniques are used. A study done at the Human Performance Lab at Adelphi University found that even though water-based heartrates were reported to be 13% lower than the land-based minimum and maximum counts, the cardiorespiratory benefits were the same as those produced by land-based exercise (Lindle, 1989). The Institute for Aerobics Research in Dallas, Texas, deducts 17 beats per minute from their projected heartrates for water exercise (Windhorst and Chossek, 1988). The 17-beat deduction was also verified in horizontal water exercise and documented by McArdle, Katch, and Katch in

Exercise, Physiology, Energy, Nutrition, and Human Performance (McArdle, 1986).

While observation has shown that heartrates generally are lower in aquatic exercise, clearly more studies are needed. Until then, heartrate information must be accepted as a basic guide rather than a hard-and-fast rule for measuring exercise intensity.

Applying Variations to the Karvonen Formula

Applying this information to the Karvonen formula, consider once again a prospective exerciser who is 40 years old and has reported a resting heartrate of 60 beats per minute (see earlier examples). The final target zone of working heartrates for *water exercise* would be from 103 to 145 beats per minute. This range is determined by subtracting 17 from the origi-

DIAGRAM 7–2 Karvonen Formula for Water Exercise

$$\frac{\begin{array}{r}220 \\ -\ \text{age}\end{array}}{\textbf{Maximal heartrate}}$$

$$\frac{\begin{array}{l}\text{Maximal heartrate} \\ -\ \text{Resting heartrate}\end{array}}{\textbf{Heartrate reserve}}$$

Heartrate reserve	Heartrate reserve
x .50 (Intensity level)	x .85 (Intensity level)
+ Resting heartrate	+ Resting heartrate
Minimum working heartrate (land-based exercise)	**Maximum working heartrate** (land-based exercise)
Minimum working heartrate (land-based exercise)	Maximum working heartrate (land-based exercise)
— 17 beats per minute	— 17 beats per minute
Minimum working heartrate for aquatic exercise	**Maximum working heartrate for aquatic exercise**

Target Zone

nal land-based figures for minimum and maximum working heartrates. Namely, the minimum working heartrate for land-based exercise was 120 beats per minute and the maximum, 162 beats per minute.

Methods of Taking Pulse Checks

Although heartrate often is discussed in terms of beats per minute, it is not actually accurate to take exercise pulse counts over a full minute, because the heart begins to slow down as soon as exercise diminishes or stops. Instead, one-minute heartrates typically are monitored by counting the beats for 6 seconds and then adding a 0 (i.e., multiply times 10).

For example, during class, the instructor would alert students of a **heartrate check** by saying, "Heartrates, go." Students would be timed for 6 seconds, at which point the instructor would say, "Stop." If a student counts 12 pulsations, that is equivalent to 120 beats per minute. A 6-second count of 16 is equivalent to 160 beats per minute. By making this simple conversion and by knowing the target zone, students can know quickly if the exercise intensity is too high or too low for them to earn cardiorespiratory benefits.

Heartrate typically is checked up to 4 times during a 45- to 60-minute class. The first check is made after the cardiovascular warm-up, when the rate might be 100 to 110 beats per minute. During the aerobic segment, working heartrates typically range from 103 to 145 when adjusted for water. A final (recovery) heartrate should be taken 5 to 10 minutes after the vigorous segment or after the cooldown. Heartrates of 110 or lower are considered safe for resuming normal activities.

When students first join, heartrates should be checked every 5 to 10 minutes simply to get participants used to the procedure and to help them understand the heartrate at which they usually work. As students become more familiar with finding the heartrate site, counting the pulse, and understanding the meaning of the resultant number, heartrates can be checked less frequently. When students are comfortable with the procedure, a heartrate check every 10 to 15 minutes is recommended.

ALTERNATE INTENSITY EVALUATION METHODS

Clearly the discussion in the first part of this appendix illustrates that many factors—from exercising in shallow water or high humidity to wearing restrictive clothing to taking medications—increase heartrate. Unfortunately, students often try to use these factors when trying to increase the intensity of a workout. But so often in aquatic exercise, the true intensity of the workout (oxygen consumption) and heartrate do not correlate at all. Because of this, students should be familiar with alternative methods of evaluating exercise intensity, which include subjective measurements such as perceived exertion, respiration rate, and the "talk test."

Rate of Perceived Exertion

While heartrate is not always a good indicator of intensity, exercisers are. Exercise physiologists working with a scientist named Gunnar Borg discovered that exercisers are able to sense their own intensity levels (Consistent Training, 1989). Participants are asked to label their activities as "Very, very light;" "Very light;" "Fairly light;" "Somewhat hard;" "Hard;" "Very hard;" or "Very, very hard." Participants are able to closely approximate their heartrate readings by how hard they perceive themselves to be working.

Based on Borg's **rate of perceived exertion (RPE)** chart (see Diagram 7–3), most exercisers should be working in the "Somewhat hard" to "Hard" range. "Very, very light" describes feelings of exertion at total rest, and "Very, very hard" describes feelings just before collapsing of exhaustion. The numbers in the left-hand column correspond to a 6-second land-based exercise heartrate.

DIAGRAM 7–3 Borg's Rate of Perceived Exertion (RPE) Chart

6	
7	Very, very light
8	
9	Very light
10	
11	Fairly light
12	
13	Somewhat hard
14	
15	Hard
16	
17	Very hard
18	
19	Very, very hard
20	

Source: Borg, G. A. V. (1982). Psychophysical Bases of Physical Exertion. *Medicine and Science in Sport and Exercise, 14,* 344–387. Used with permission.

Pollock, Wilmore, and Fox found that ratings of 12 to 13 are equal to about 60% of maximal heartrate reserve, while 16 is equal to about 90% of maximal heartrate reserve (Pollock et al., 1984). Participants working in the "Somewhat hard" to "Hard" range during the aerobic phase of the class will be working in the 60% to 90% range of maximal heartrate reserve.

Borg found that the RPE scale correlated very highly with heartrate, **ventilation,** oxygen consumption, and blood lactate concentration (Borg, 1982). Since it has already been shown that heartrate is not a very reliable measure of exertion in aquatic exercise, it seems that the RPE method may work well not

DIAGRAM 7–4 American College of Sports Medicine (ACSM) Rate of Perceived Exertion (RPE) Chart

0	Nothing
0.5	Very, very light (just noticeable)
1.0	Very light
2	Light (weak)
3	Moderate
4	Somewhat hard
5	Heavy (strong)
6	
7	Very heavy
8	
9	
10	Very, very heavy (almost max)

Source: Consistent Training, 1989

only for aquatic exercisers but also for special populations using medications.

The ACSM revised the RPE scale in 1986 making it simpler for participants to use (see Diagram 7–4). This scale goes from 0, which is "Nothing," to 10, which is "Very, very heavy." It provides more verbal descriptions for participants to rate their exertion levels.

Participants in water exercise sometimes perceive their exertion to be somewhat lower because of the cooling effect and the enjoyment of the water. This is not the case, however. The RPE method can be a reliable guide to measuring intensity in cardiovascular activity. In fact, some exercise professionals find it the most useful indicator of workout intensity. Some aquatic exercise instructors combine heartrate response and RPE methods. They have participants get used to taking a pulse during exercise and relating how they feel during that workout. After a few weeks of pulse checks,

participants are able to perceive their own levels of intensity without checking pulses.

Respiration Rate

In order for an exerciser to get extra oxygen, he or she must take more breaths per minute. If the **respiration rate** (or breaths per minute) during activity does not increase, the exercise is not intense enough. Measuring respiration rate is a technique to determine just the lower limit (minimum working heartrate) of intensity. Using respiration rate to determine exercise intensity normally is done in conjunction with another method, such as heartrate or RPE, for monitoring intensity.

"Talk Test"

The so-called **"talk test"** is very simple: If participants cannot talk when they are exercising, it means they are working too hard. If they are working out so strenuously that they cannot visit with the person next to them, it means the exercise is no longer aerobic. Participants should be able to breathe comfortably and deeply during the entire workout. If they are short of breath, panting, or gasping and are unable to talk, their workout is too intense. Rather than burning fat and carbohydrate calories, they are burning protein. The "talk test" monitors only the top end of the target zone (maximum working heartrate).

Overexertion

If exercisers experience pain during any workout, they should stop exercising, walk slowly in place, and inform their instructor. Instructors should look out for participants who display any of the following signs of **overexertion:**
- nausea
- extreme weakness
- profuse sweating
- a red face
- breathlessness

- excessive fatigue
- chest pain or discomfort
- lightheadedness or dizziness
- focused musculoskeletal discomfort
- ataxic (unsteady) gait
- confusion

It is important that the aquatic exerciser understands the sources of fatigue so that the symptoms listed above can be eliminated.

Hyperthermia

Hyperthermia is the overheating of the body, which can happen in warm water or pool environments with very little circulation. The participant feels an overall loss of energy.

Glycogen Depletion

Glycogen depletion causes graduated and overall fatigue. Participants should keep the workout at low to moderate intensity for short periods and gradually overload to avoid glycogen depletion.

Musculoskeletal Fatigue

Musculoskeletal fatigue often is recognized by pain in a bone, joint, or muscle. Overdoing any one exercise movement can cause musculoskeletal fatigue.

Lactic Acid Accumulation

Lactic acid accumulation comes on relatively quickly and usually is focused in one particular muscle group. It can be avoided by reducing workout duration and intensity and by varying the exercise.

WATER AS A
WORKOUT
MEDIUM

Chapter Eight

GENERAL INFORMATION

Because of water's unique properties, water-based exercise provides somewhat different benefits than land-based exercise. To allow for those properties, modifications need to be made before using land-based exercises.

Water Resistance

Water resistance is the power of fluid to oppose an exercise movement. Water has approximately 12 times the resistance of air. That resistance may slow the exerciser down, but it gives him or her some tremendous benefits.

Movement Speed

Movement speed refers to the quickness of an exercise motion. When moving in the water, exercisers need to modify the pace of movements to allow for water resistance. The speed must be adjusted so movements are ac-complished without jerking or compromising alignment and use a full range of motion. Movements always should be controlled. If the exercise being done causes the body to move out of alignment in an uncontrolled fashion, it is too fast. The speed at which one would jog on land is not the speed at which one should jog in water. Likewise, the speed of kicks done on land should not be the same for kicks done in the water. Moving through the water with ballistic, land-based speed movements can cause injuries to the joints and ligaments.

Toning Potential

Water resistance, while slowing an exer-ciser down, also provides excellent benefits. When moving through water, one not only re-ceives cardiovascular benefits (by pushing the heartrate or perceived exertion level up into the target zone); one also receives toning ben-efits not available on land. Water resistance acts with equalized pressure on all submerged body parts. Any time a limb is moved through the water, additional toning occurs because of water resistance.

Muscle Balance

Muscle balance is another benefit of working in water. Almost all joints in the body have some muscles that flex them and other muscles that extend them. The two muscles that work a joint (flex and extend) are generally thought of as a pair, or muscle pair. The **flexors** almost always are stronger than the extensors. The **extensors** generally work with gravity, which does the work for them; thus, extensors usually are not well developed. If exercise programs contribute to naturally occurring muscle imbalance, injury could result, especially if those joints are weight bearing.

When participants exercise in water, they receive equalized muscle balance that is not available through any other medium. Due to the flotation effect of water, a person working in water uses the iliopsoas (hip flexor) muscles when lifting (kicking forward) the leg and gets the additional benefit (not received on land) of using the gluteals and hamstrings when lowering the leg back through the water. The same is true with the bicep and tricep muscle pair and most other muscle pairs in the body. The tricep gets virtually no work during arm extensions in land-based exercises (gravity does the work). Water resistance, however, forces the tricep to work when doing arm extensions. Muscle balance is a tremendous benefit of water exercise.

Energy Expenditure

A water workout gives a greater **energy expenditure** than a similar land-based exercise. When walking on land, each step recruits a certain amount of muscle fibers. Each muscle fiber needs a certain amount of oxygen to keep it going. **Oxygen consumption** correlates with energy and caloric consumption. When the same walking is done in water, more muscle

fibers need to be recruited for each step taken. That means more oxygen is used, and there is greater energy and caloric expenditure.

Water-based exercise achieves a workout intensity similar to that of land-based exercise with less heart stress. One function of the heart is to help the body dissipate heat. If the heart has to work at dissipating heat at the same time it is working to deliver oxygen to muscles, it can become overloaded and work at a higher rate (beats per minute) than necessary for cardiovascular fitness. If the body is cooled by water and the heart does not have to work at dissipating heat, it can concentrate on simply supplying oxygen to the muscles. Thus, a similar workout intensity is achieved while maintaining a lower heartrate.

Arm Movements

Arm movements in aquatic exercise can be used in much the same way they are used on land: for variety and fun, for balance, for coordination improvement, and for adding intensity to the workout. In addition, arm movements can be used for other purposes more particularly suited to aquatic exercise.

Arm movements can help the body move through water. By pressing the hands from front to back, the exerciser is propelled forward. By starting with the arms to the right and sweeping left, the participant slides to the right. If the hands are pushed straight down, the body will spring up. Each of these movements can be reversed for the opposite effect.

The benefit of using arms to assist with movement in the water becomes apparent when the body presents a large surface area and is, therefore, resistant to the movement. For example, when a participant is facing straight forward and attempts to jump ahead through the water, the frontal resistance of the body is at its greatest. It is extremely difficult to accomplish this movement without using the arms. As one jogs through the water, more territory can be covered if arms are added to the movement to help pull the body forward.

Changing directions can produce swirls of water, which make movement more difficult. Appropriate arm movements can assist the body in accomplishing direction changes.

In the water, when the body is at a standstill, it takes more effort to put it into motion than it does to maintain a standstill. Upper-body movements can add to the total effort and make it possible to overcome this resistance.

All the while arms are being used in the water for balance, coordination, movement assists, or fun, they are also developing upper-body muscular endurance and strength. Pushing, pulling, sweeping, flicking, and lifting all work muscles in the upper and lower arms, the shoulders, the chest, the abdominals, and the upper and lower back. If arms are kept submerged while executing the movements, the potential for gains is greater, because water resistance acts like weights or bands to increase the difficulty of the exercise. Although some land-based movements are advantageous for the students and assure that joints move through a full range of motion, the benefits of using arms in the water to increase the workload should not be overlooked.

The position of the hands and upper body can increase or decrease the intensity of various exercises. Because swimming programs train people to move efficiently in water, it is sometimes difficult for students to learn to purposely increase water resistance for a more difficult workout.

Presenting a small surface area against the water makes it easier to perform arm movements. For example, turning the hands so they slice through the water requires less upper body effort than if the hands are flattened to the direction of the movement. By choosing the appropriate hand position for each movement, aquatic exercisers can do one movement but develop different degrees of conditioning, depending on the workload they place on the muscle.

In addition to affecting the particular muscles in use, arm movements can affect the cardiorespiratory demands on the body during exercise. Greater demand is placed on the heart and lungs as they work harder to meet the muscles' need for oxygen, nutrients, and waste removal. This is accomplished simply by adding arm movements rather than letting arms hang in the water. Cardiorespiratory conditioning can be boosted even further by cupping or flattening the hands as the arms move through the water.

Water Buoyancy and Cushioning

The cushioning effect is another benefit of exercise in the water. Because of the 90% apparent weight loss in shoulder-depth water, participants can exercise with less biomechanical stress during each footstrike or **impact.** This allows them to exercise longer and more frequently and to gain more benefits without the likelihood of injury.

POOL CONDITIONS

Knowledge about the area where water exercise classes meet helps ensure a safe program for participants. Different programs are suited ideally to different pool environments. Being aware of the factors that are *not* ideal allows the instructor or student to modify conditions and compensate for inadequacies. **Pool conditions,** such as the surface of the pool bottom, the water temperature, and water depth all affect the safety of a workout.

A **pool bottom** should have a smooth but nonslippery surface. It should be marked plainly and conspicuously to indicate depth, with specific markings at break points. The proper grate on the drain cover should be screwed in.

Water temperature is of utmost importance. For high-intensity workouts with healthy, fit individuals who need to dissipate heat, ideal pool temperatures should be 80 to 83 degrees Fahrenheit. In water below 80 degrees, participants should increase the time spent in the warm-up phase before moving on to full-range-of-motion, high-level aerobic activity.

While cool temperatures present one set of difficulties, pools with temperatures over 85 degrees present another potential risk, that of overheating. Overheating may result when warm water interferes with heat dissipation, the body's ability to radiate excess heat to a cooler environment. *Caution is needed.* Some pools are heated to over 90 degrees. These pools should not be used for aerobic activities.

The ideal **water depth** for most aquatic exercisers is midriff or armpit level. This water depth allows participants to use their arms, which provides additional body toning. They also experience enough body weight to control their movements, keep a good sense of balance, and maintain reasonable footing during the exercises. Midriff to armpit water depth also allows the exerciser to experience enough body weight to make the workout a challenge and achieve the intensity needed to produce cardiovascular benefits. At that depth, however, participants can experience enough buoyancy to protect their joints, ligaments, and tendons from the stress of high impact.

KEY WORDS

Water resistance	Oxygen consumption	Impact
Movement speed	Water buoyancy	Pool bottom
Muscle balance	Flexors	Water temperature
Energy expenditure	Extensors	Water depth

SUMMARY

- Water has approximately 12 times the resistance of air.
- When moving in the water, exercisers need to modify the pace of movements to allow for the water resistance.
- Water resistance, while slowing an exerciser down, also provides excellent benefits.
- Muscle balance is a benefit of working in water.
- A water workout can give a greater energy expenditure than a similar land-based exercise.
- Water-based exercise can achieve a workout intensity similar to that of land-based exercise with less heart stress.
- Arm movements in the aquatic exercise can be used in much the same way they are used on land: for variety and fun, for balance, for coordination improvement, and to add intensity.
- Arm movements also can be used for purposes more particularly suited to aquatic exercise.
- Because of the 90% apparent weight loss in shoulder-depth water, participants can exercise with less biomechanical stress during each footstrike or impact.
- Knowledge about the area where water exercise classes meet helps ensure a safe program for participants.
- For high-intensity workouts with healthy, fit individuals who need to dissipate heat, the ideal pool temperature should be 80 to 83 Fahrenheit.
- The ideal water depth for most aquatic exercisers is to the midriff or the armpit.

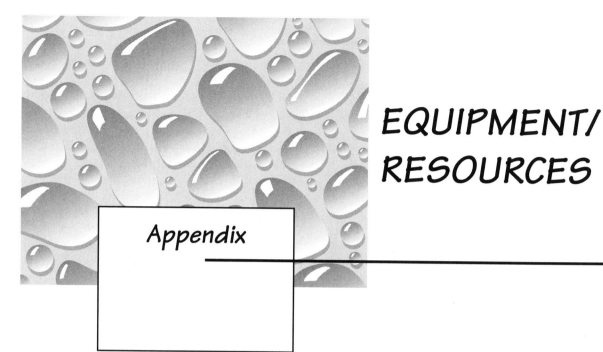

EQUIPMENT/ RESOURCES

Appendix

EQUIPMENT INFORMATION

Equipment Principles

All equipment is based on one or more of three basic principles: **buoyancy, weight,** or **resistance.** Unless equipment is designed for therapeutic use or to keep a person buoyant in deep water, it is designed to inhibit movement (resistance), increase weight, or increase the force needed for a movement (buoyancy), thereby increasing the intensity. Weights increase impact, muscular endurance, and muscular strength. Buoyant equipment usually lessens impact and increases muscular strength and endurance. Resistant equipment does not affect impact but increases muscular endurance and strength.

Precautions and Contraindications

Exercisers using equipment should follow specific guidelines, regardless of whether buoyant, resistant, or weighted equipment is used. The following are **precautions,** or measures to guard against injuries:

1. *Progressive overload:* When adding equipment, the concept of gradual overload should be applied in terms of intensity, frequency, and duration. Intensity can be increased in a number of ways. Using equipment, a participant should begin with a light piece and gradually progress to a heavy piece. An example would be to begin with webbed gloves, progress to Frisbees, and after adaptation occurs, progress to Hydro-Tone. In terms of duration, equipment should be added only for 5 to 10 minutes the first day. As students adapt to the equipment, time can be increased. In the beginning, equipment should be used only once or twice a week. Participants can increase the frequency gradually as adaptation occurs.
2. *Begin slowly:* Each time equipment is used, participants should begin slowly and gradually add more forceful movements. They also should begin using short levers and gradually progress to longer levers and more intense moves.

Short levers also should be used for faster movements and long levers reserved for slower movements. Using long levers quickly can damage the soft tissue around joints.

3. *Muscle balance:* The muscles on each side of a joint should be worked equally to assure muscle balance during a workout. In order to ensure muscle balance, the exerciser should apply equal force in both directions of the movement.

4. *Keep joints "soft":* Full extensions of the knees, shoulders, elbows, and wrists should be eliminated. These joints should always be "soft," or slightly flexed, to prevent injury.

5. *Keep the equipment in the water:* Moves using aquatic exercise equipment should be accomplished completely in the water. Eliminate in-and-out-of-the-water types of moves, as they can severely compromise joints and muscles.

6. *Stretch what you strengthen:* While flexibility is important in all types of programs, stretching is even more vital when equipment is used. Any muscles that are worked with equipment should be stretched at the end of the program.

7. *Move toward and away from the body center:* To reduce strain on ligaments and tendons in the shoulders, elbows, knees, and hips, use moves such as bicep curls or sidekicks that move toward and away from the body center. Extensive movements on the periphery of the body, such as arm circles or leg circles, can cause strain.

8. *Always "place" the piece of equipment:* Participants sometimes fling equipment, especially if the movement is performed too quickly. Students should visualize where the piece of equipment will be at the end of the move and "place" it there. For safety purposes, participants should keep a firm grip on the equipment so it stays with them and does not hit other body parts or other individuals. Students should always know where the equipment is going.

9. *Use equipment only after the warm-up:* Before adding equipment, allow the body to warm up, supplying muscles with oxygenated blood and lubricating the joints.

10. *Use full range of motion:* Participants often cut movements short when they tire. If the movement is not brought back to its beginning position, it results in ineffective work and muscle shortening. **Full range of motion** must be stressed.

11. *Use proper alignment:* Alignment is important in all programs and even more important when using equipment. Improper use of equipment can easily cause injuries to students. Exercisers should have complete control over movements with equipment.

Population Contraindications

Without a medical professional's guidance, some special populations should not use equipment. Participants with high blood pressure, heart disease, arthritis, or other joint problems should not use equipment. Participants with back or knee problems or pregnant women should have medical approval before attempting to use equipment that increases the intensity of the program.

AQUATIC EXERCISE ASSOCIATION

The Aquatic Exercise Association is an international association of aquatic professions. The Association was founded by Ruth Sova in 1986. For further information about the topics covered in this book, aquatic equipment, certification, videotapes, workshops, and seminars, write to:

Aquatic Exercise Association
P.O. Box 497
Port Washington, WI 53074

REFERENCES

AEA Heart Rate Study. (1987, September). *The AKWA Letter, 2* (3), p. 7.

Aerobic and Fitness Association of America. (1982). *Aerobics: Theory and Practice.* Atlanta: Author.

Aldridge, M. (1990, May). Step. *Fitness Management,* pp. 32-38.

American Cancer Society. (1988). *Facts on Skin Cancer.*

American College of Sports Medicine. (1990a, July). ACSM Guidelines for Fitness Updated. *Running & Fitnews, 8,* 1.

American College of Sports Medicine. (1990b). *ACSM Position Stand: The Recommended Quantity and Quality of Exercise for Developing and Maintaining Cardiorespiratory and Muscular Fitness in Healthy Adults.* Indianapolis: Author.

American College of Sports Medicine. (1982). *Guidelines for Graded Exercise Testing and Exercise Prescription.* Indianapolis: Author.

American Heart Association. (1989). *1989 Heart Facts.* Dallas: Author.

Artal, R., Friedman, M. J., & McNitt-Gray, J. (1990, September). Orthopedic Problems in Pregnancy. *The Physician and Sportsmedicine, 18* (9), 93–100.

Beasley, R. L. (1989, January). Aquatic Exercise. *Sports Medicine Digest,* pp. 1–3.

Borg, G. A. V. (1982). Pyschophysical Bases of Physical Exertion. *Medicine and Science in Sport and Exercise, 14,* 377–387.

Brehm, B. A. (1990, August). Why Exercise Should Be A Lifelong Priority. *Fitness Management,* p. 20.

Brehm, B. A. (1990, May). Making an Impact on Bone Density. *Fitness Management,* p. 14.

Chase, S. (1977). *Moving to Win—The Physics of Sports.*

Chossek V., Delzeit, L., Lindle, J., Sova, R., & Windhorst, M. (1990). *Aquatic Concepts.* Port Washington, WI: Aquatic Exercise Association.

Chossek, V. (1988, January). AKWA Network: In my Opinion. *The AKWA Letter, 1* (5), 4.

Chrisman, D. C. (1983). *Body Recall* (2nd ed.). Berea, KY: Berea College Press.

Cirullo, J. (1989, May). Part I: Attaining and Maintaining a Healthy Back Through Wise Water Work. *The AKWA Letter, 3* (1), 1.

Cirullo, J. (1989, July). Part II: Attaining and Maintaining a Healthy Back Through Wise Water Work. *The AKWA Letter, 3* (2), 5–6.

Cisar, C. J., & Kravitz, L. (1989, January). Interval Training. *IDEA Today,* pp. 13–17.

Close, S. (1990). Equipment and Props for Exercise. *Reebok Instructor News, 3* (4), 7.

Conrad, C. C. (1979, February). Why Your Organization Should Consider Starting a Physical Fitness Program. *TRAINING, The Magazine of Human Resources Development,* pp. 30–31.

Consistent Training. (1989, Fall). *The Pursuit of Excellence, 4* (3), 1–2.

Cooper, K. (1982). *The Aerobics Program for Total Well-Being.* New York: Bantam Books.

Couzens, G. S. (1989, March). Plunging into Therapy. *Newsday,* p. 11.

DeCluitt, M. M. (1988, July). Water Exercise for Older Bodies. *The AKWA Letter, 2* (2), 10.

Dougan, T. (1989, July). Silver Splash: A Water Workout for Seniors. *The AKWA Letter, 3* (2), 12–13.

Essert, M. B. (1989, May). Water Walking. *The AKWA Letter, 3* (1), 3.

Evans, B., Cureton, K., & Purvis, J. (1978). Metabolic and Circulatory Responses to Walking and Jogging in Water. *Research Quarterly, 49* (4), 442–449.

Every Body in the Pool. (1989, September). *The Pursuit of Excellence, 4* (4), 1–2.

Exercising in Hot Weather. (1989, July). *The AKWA Letter, 3,* (2), 1.

Flatten, K., Wilhite, B., & Reyes-Watson, E. (1988). *Exercise Activities for the Elderly*. New York: Springer.

Francis, L., & Francis, P. (1990). Step Training. *Reebok Instructor News, 3* (5), 12.

Growing Up Fit. (1989, November/December). *IDEA Today*, p. 7.

Herman, E. (1989, December 11). Saving Your Skin. *Pool and Spa News*, pp. 46–47.

Horstmeyer, B. (1989a, March). Aquatics for Expectant Mothers. *The AKWA Letter, 2* (6), 1.

Horstmeyer, B. (1989b). *Perinatal Certification Instructor's Manual*. Milwaukee, WI: Maternity Fitness.

Huttner, B. (1988, November). Aquatic Exercise Equipment: Flugels. *The AKWA Letter, 2* (4), 3.

Increase in Bone Density? (1988, March). *Fitness Management*, 6.

Institute for Aerobics Research. (1981). Management of Exercise and Fitness Programs. Dallas: The Aerobics Center.

Johnson, B. L. et al. (1977). Comparison of Oxygen Uptake and Heart Rate During Exercises on Land and in Water. *Physical Therapy, 57* (3), 273–278.

Kendall, F. P., Kendall, F., & Wadsworth, P. (1971). Muscle Testing & Function. Baltimore: Williams and Wilkins.

Koszuta, L. (1988, September). Splash On By. *Walking Magazine*, pp. 65, 66, 68, 70.

Lindle, J. (1989). Water Exercise Research. *The AKWA Letter, 3* (4), 11, 13.

Luttgens, M., & Wells, L. (1982). *Kinesiology—Scientific Basis of Human Motion* (7th ed.). Philidelphia: W. B. Saunders.

McArdle, W., Katch, F., & Katch, V. (1986). *Exercise Physiology, Energy, Nutrition, and Human Performance*. Philadelphia: Lea and Febiger.

McWaters, G. (1988). *How the Older Become Younger and the Impaired Become Repaired*. Birmingham, AL.

Mitchell, T. (1989, May). The Use of Props in Water Exercise for Muscle Conditioning. *The AKWA Letter, 3* (1), 6.

Monroe, E. (1988, July). The Sun and Your Skin. *The AKWA Letter, 2,* (2), 7–9.

Murphy, J. (1985, July). Shopwalk. *Sports Illustrated*, p. 12.

Nelson, A. T. (1989, April). Workshop on Aquatic Circuit Training. International Aquatic Fitness Conference, Chicago, IL.

Nelson, A. T. (1989, April). Workshop on Deep Water Fitness. International Aquatic Fitness Conference, Chicago, IL.

Osinski, A. (1990, February). The Complete Aquatic Guide. *Parks & Recreation*, pp. 36–43.

Osinski, A. (1989, Spring). Water Running. *National Aquatics Journal*, pp. 3-6.

Osinski, A. (1988, September). Water Myths. *The AKWA Letter, 2* (3), 1.

Pitts, E. H. (1990c, July). Getting Strong After Age 90. *Fitness Management*, p. 12.

Pollock, M. L. et al. (1982). Comparison of Methods for Determining Exercise Training Intensity for Cardiac Patients and Healthy Adults. *Advanced Cardiology, 31,* 129–133.

Pollock, M. L., Wilmore, J. H., & Fox, S. M. (1984). *Exercise in Health and Disease*. Philadelphia: W. B. Saunders.

Research Abstracts. (1990). *Reebok Instructor News, 3* (4), 4.

Research Project. (1988, May). *The AKWA Letter, 2* (1), 6.

Rikli, R., & McManis, B. (1990, September). Effects of Exercise on Bone Mineral Content in Postmenopausal Women. *Research Quarterly for Exercise and Sport, 61* (3), 243–249.

Riposo, D. (1990). *Fitness Concepts*. Port Washington, WI: Aquatic Exercise Association.

Riposo, D. (1985). *America's Certification Trainers Manual.* Port Washington, WI: The Fitness Firm.

Robbins, G. et al. (1989). *The Wellness Way of Life.* Dubuque, IA: Wm. C. Brown.

See, J. (1990, January). Aqua Power Aerobics. *The AKWA Letter, 3* (5), 1.

Seibert, G. R. (1990, July). Here Come the Kids, Are You Ready? *Fitness Management,* p. 22.

Shortley, G., & Williams, D. (1965). *Elements of Physics.* Englewood Cliffs, NJ: Prentice Hall.

Sova, R. (1990a, May). Heartrates in Aquatic Exercise. *IDEA Today,* p. 9.

Sova, R. (1989a, July). Body Alignment: How to Maintain It. *The AKWA Letter, 3* (2), 10.

Sova, R. (1989b, July). Exercising in Hot Weather. *The AKWA Letter, 3* (2), p. 6.

Special Considerations for Special Seniors. (1990). *Reebok Instructor News, 3* (4), 8.

Spitzer, T. A. et al. (1989). *A Comparison of Selected Training Responses to Water Aerobics and Low-Impact Aerobics.* Prepared by Boise State University; Idaho Sports Medicine Institute; and Indiana State University.

Spodnik, J. O., & Cogan, D. P. (1989). *The 35-Plus Good Health Guide for Women.* New York: Harper and Row.

Strovas, J. (1990, September). 90-year-olds Increase Strength Dramatically. *The Physician and Sportsmedicine, 18* (9), 26.

U.S. Department of Agriculture and Department of Health and Human Services (1979). *Nutrition and Your Health, Dietary Guidelines for Americans.* Washington, DC: Authors.

U.S. Department of Health and Human Services (1984). *What You Need to Know About Cancer of the Skin.* Washington, DC: National Cancer Institute.

VanCamp, G., & Boyer, B. (1989, May). Exercise Guidelines for the Elderly. *The Physician and Sportsmedicine, 17* (5), 14-16.

Vickery, S. R., Cureton, K. J., & Langstaff, J. L. (1983, March). Heart Rate and Energy Expenditure During Aqua Dynamics. *The Physician and Sportsmedicine, 11* (3), 67-72.

Walters, J. (1990, April). Handout from Children's Creative Movement Workshop. International Aquatic Fitness Conference, Chicago, IL.

Warm Up: It Pays Dividends. (1987, July). *The AKWA Letter, 1* (2), 1.

Water Exercise: A Better Fat Burner. (1988, January). *The AKWA Letter, 1* (5), 5.

Weider, J. (1990, October). Quality Time. *Shape,* p. 7.

Welch, D. (1989, July). Water Dancing. *Health,* pp. 46-51.

Wigglesworth, J. K. et al. (1990, September). Aquatic Exercise Research: The Effect of Water Exercise on Various Parameters of Physical Fitness. *The AKWA Letter, 4* (3), 3.

Windhorst, M., & Chossek, V. (1988). *Aquatic Exercise Association Manual.* Port Washington, WI: Aquatic Exercise Association.

Young, T. (1990). *Older Adult Exercise Manual* (4th ed.). Lansing, KS: Young Enterprises.

NOTES

NOTES

NOTES